Essential Keyboard Repertoire
Volume 8

95 Early/Late Intermediate Miniatures
One or Two Pages in Length

Baroque to Modern

Selected and Edited by
Maurice Hinson

Second Edition
Copyright © MCMXCVI by Alfred Publishing Co., Inc.
All rights reserved. Printed in USA.

Cover design: Martha Widmann   Art direction: Ted Engelbart
Cover: *The Bassin des Tuileries: Afternoon Sun*, 1900
by Camille Pissarro (French, 1830–1903)
Oil on canvas (73 x 92 cm)
The Israel Museum, Jerusalem

ESSENTIAL KEYBOARD REPERTOIRE
95 Early/Late Intermediate Miniatures One or Two Pages in Length

Selected and Edited by Maurice Hinson

CONTENTS

	Page
Foreword	2
The Intermediate-Level Student	3
Editing	3
Contents Listed by Composer	3
Contents Listed by Title	5
Contents Listed by Level	
Early Intermediate	7
Intermediate	7
Late Intermediate	8

This edition is dedicated to Dr. Donald Massingale, with admiration and appreciation.
Maurice Hinson

Foreword

Piano literature contains some wonderful and exciting miniatures for the intermediate student. For the purposes of this volume, a miniature is a piece no longer than two pages. Some of the greatest composers wrote short pieces that reinforce essential elements of musicianship and technique. These miniatures have proven to be effective teaching pieces throughout the years since they were written.

The intermediate piano repertoire is so extensive that it is frequently difficult for the teacher and student to locate some of these attractive miniatures. *Essential Keyboard Repertoire: 95 Early/Late Intermediate Miniatures, One or Two Pages in Length* is designed to assist both teacher and student with this problem. Some of these miniatures are well known, while others may not be so familiar. All contain the following essential characteristics:

1. Interesting melodies, rhythm and harmonies
2. Technical accessibility
3. Carefully planned design and formal structure
4. Exceptional aesthetic value

These miniatures are easily learned by today's busy students. The editor prefers assigning two or three miniatures rather than one large work. Students often prefer the variety provided by several miniatures over one long repertoire piece.

In addition to use in the formal lesson, this collection can be used (1) as a sight-reading supplement for more advanced students, (2) by the pianist for his or her enjoyment, (3) by the pianist performing at receptions and other social events, and (4) for auditions and competition.

The Intermediate-Level Student

The intermediate level is a crucial period in the development of a pianist. It encompasses the period of time when a student is nearing completion of beginning method books but is not quite ready to move on to advanced works by the great composers. Individual students reach this level at different rates, depending on their ability, age and previous experience. To facilitate easy use, this collection is divided into three levels: *early intermediate*, *intermediate* and *late intermediate*.

Students at the early-intermediate level should be able to play the scales of C, G, D and F major, plus D and A minor. These students should also be able to perform musically the pieces in J. S. Bach's *Anna Magdalena Notebook* or similar pieces of equivalent difficulty. Material for this level should approximate *Level 3* of *Alfred's Basic Piano Library*.

Students at the *intermediate* level should be able to play the scales of C, G, D, F and B-flat major, plus D, A, E and G minor. At this level, students should be able to play some of the easier dances in J. S. Bach's *Notebook for W. F. Bach*, easier dances by Beethoven and other pieces of equivalent difficulty. The repertoire and minimum technical requirements for this level approximate *Level 4* of *Alfred's Basic Piano Library*.

Students at the *late-intermediate* level should be able to play the scales of C, G, D, A, E, F, B-flat, E-flat and A-flat major, plus A, D, E, G, B, C, F-sharp and C-sharp minor. Appropriate repertoire for this level should approximate *Levels 5–6* of *Alfred's Basic Piano Library* or more difficult works such as selected *Two-Part Inventions* of J. S. Bach and *Sonatinas* of Kuhlau.

The editor hopes that you will find much pleasure in playing these attractive miniatures, and will thereby develop a fond appreciation for this repertoire.

Editing

Great care has been given to the layout and engraving of this music. Each piece appears in its original form; notes have not been added or removed, unless stated otherwise. When articulation, notes, pedal, dynamics or interpretive indications have been added by the editor, they are always identified in footnotes or parenthetically. Either more or less pedal may be used than is indicated in some pieces, depending on room acoustics, the sound of the instrument and the personality of the player. Fingerings are based on modern teaching principles and are editorial. Measures are numbered for easy reference. The indications *f*–*mp* (or other dynamics) mean that the section is to be played forte the first time and mezzo piano on the repeat.

Contents Listed by Composer

Anonymous
Musette in D Major, BWV Anh. 126,
   from *Anna Magdalena Bach Klavierbüchlein*, 1725 9

Bach, Carl Philipp Emanuel
Fantasia in G Major, Wq. 117:8 94
Solfeggio in C Minor, Wq. 117:2 48

Bach, Johann Christian
Tempo Giusto 52

Bach, Johann Christoph Friedrich
Menuett in G Major 18
Moderato in C Major 19

Bach, Johann Sebastian
Aria in D Minor, BWV 515,
   from *Anna Magdalena Bach Klavierbüchlein*, 1725 10
Gavotte II in D Major, BWV 811,
   from *English Suite No. 6* 93
March in E-flat Major, BWV Anh. 127,
   from *Anna Magdalena Bach Klavierbüchlein*, 1725 44

Bach, Wilhelm Friedemann
Minuet in G Major 17

Backer-Grøndahl, Agathe
Song of Youth, Op. 45, No. 1 67

Bartók, Béla
Above the Tree, Under the Tree, Sz. 42:45 82
Dance Song, Sz. 42:49 83
Little Scherzo, Sz. 52:82 34
Parsley and Celery, Sz. 42:21 33
Swineherd's Dance, Sz. 52:77 35

Beethoven, Ludwig van
Bagatelle in A Major, Op. 119, No. 10 28
German Dance in F Major, WoO 42, No. 1 29
Minuet in E-flat Major, WoO 10, No. 3 58

Brahms, Johannes
Waltz in E Major, Op. 39, No. 2 108

Chaminade, Cécile
Orientale, Op. 123, No. 9 70

Chopin, Frédéric
Bourrée II in A Major, KK 1404 60
Gallop Marquis, KKp 1240a 61
Prelude in A Major, Op. 28, No. 7 62
Prelude in C Minor, Op. 28, No. 20 100

Czerný, Joseph
Cossack Dance 30

Debussy, Claude
Album Leaf, L. 133 114
La fille aux cheveux de lin
   (The Girl with the Flaxen Hair), L. 117:8 116

Foster, Stephen C.
Soirée Polka 106

Friedman, Ignacy
Fairy Tale Princess, The, Op. 76, No. 8 130

Gambarini, Elisabetta de
Tambourin in F Major 47

Goedicke, Alexander
In a Quiet Mood 80

Granados, Enrique
Bell of the Afternoon, The, from *Bocetos* 120
Poetic Valse No. 5 77
Poetic Valse No. 6 122

Grieg, Edvard
Patriotic Song, Op. 12, No. 8 68

Gurlitt, Cornelius
Bolero 102

Handel, George Frideric
Gigue in D Minor from *Suite No. 4* 46
Menuett in C Minor 16

Hässler, Johann Wilhelm
Ecossaise in G Major 21

Haydn, Franz Joseph
Gypsy Dance, Hob. IX:28/6 20
Vivace in D Major, Hob. I:92/4 50

Heller, Stephen
Gypsies, Op. 138, No. 19 104

Indy, Vincent d'
Bourrée en Rondeau 112

Kabalevsky, Dmitri
By the Campfire, Op. 3/86, No. 6 138
Dance on the Lawn, Op. 27, No. 11 88
Hopping, Op. 39, No. 18 37
Merry Tune, A, Op. 89, No. 26 38
Night on the River, Op. 27, No. 4 39
Old Dance, An, Op. 27, No. 7 90
Waltz, Op. 27, No. 1 40
Warlike Song, A, Op. 89, No. 30 91
Who Will Win the Argument?, Op. 88, No. 2 140

Khachaturian, Aram
Bedtime Story 86
Cat on a Swing 136
Skipping 36

Kirchner, Theodor
Catch Me If You Can!, Op. 55, No. 23 66

Kullak, Theodor
Grandmother Tells a Ghost Story, Op. 81, No. 3 64

Liszt, Franz
Bell Tolls, The, S. 238 101

MacDowell, Edward
To a Wild Rose, Op. 51, No. 1 72

Maykapar, Samuel
Blacksmith, The, Op. 8, No. 5 124
Echo in the Mountains, Op. 28, No. 19 78

Mendelssohn, Felix
Song without Words, Op. 30, No. 3 96

Mozart, Leopold
Bourrée in C Minor 14

Mozart, Wolfgang Amadeus
Bread and Butter 23
Klavierstück in F Major (Piano Piece), K. 33b 56

Myslivecek, Josef
Divertimento No. I in F Major 54

Neefe, Christian Gottlob
Kanzonette in C Major 22

Nielsen, Carl
Danish Folk Tune, Op. 3, No. 1 118

Oesten, Theodore
Sound of the Hunting Horn, The 32

Prokofiev, Sergei
March, Op. 65, No. 10 84

Rameau, Jean-Philippe
Le Lardon—Menuet 43

Rebikov, Vladimir
Lame Witch Lurking in the Forest, The,
     Op. 31, No. 9 76

Reinagle, Alexander
Allegro in B-flat Major 24
Jigg in A Major 57
Presto in F Major 25

Satie, Erik
Tango, The (Endless) 119

Scarlatti, Domenico
Aria in D Minor, K. 32 12
Sonata in G Major, K. 431 11

Schmitt, Florent
Valse Viennoise (Viennese Waltz), Op. 32, No. 8 126

Schubert, Franz
German Dance in B-flat Major, D. 783, No. 7 59
Waltz in B Minor, D. 145:6 95

Schumann, Robert
Traümerei (Dreaming), Op. 15, No. 7 98

Scriabin, Alexander
Prelude in G Minor, Op. 11, No. 22 128

Shostakovich, Dmitri
Happy Birthday, Op. 69, No. 7 142
Russian Menuet 41

Sibelius, Jean
Valsette, Op. 40, No. 1 74

Tchaikovsky, Peter Ilyich
Song of the Lark, Op. 39, No. 22 110

Tcherepnin, Alexander
Bagatelle, Op. 5, No. 1 132
Chinese March 134
Jade Wheel Turns in the Dew, The 135

Türk, Daniel Gottlob
Having Fun Crossing Hands 26
Those Broken Octaves! 27

Wagner, Richard
Polka 63

Weber, Carl Maria von
Ballett in F Major 31

Contents Listed by Title

Above the Tree, Under the Tree, Sz. 42:45
Bartók 82

Album Leaf, L. 133
Debussy 114

Allegro in B-flat Major
Reinagle 24

Aria in D Minor, BWV 515,
from *Anna Magdalena Bach Klavierbüchlein*, 1725
Bach, J. S. 10

Aria in D Minor, K. 32
Scarlatti, D. 12

Bagatelle in A Major, Op. 119, No. 10
Beethoven 28

Bagatelle, Op. 5, No. 1
Tcherepnin 132

Ballett in F Major
Weber 31

Bedtime Story
Khachaturian 86

Bell of the Afternoon, The, from *Bocetos*
Granados 120

Bell Tolls, The, S. 238
Liszt 101

Blacksmith, The, Op. 8, No. 5
Maykapar 124

Bolero
Gurlitt 102

Bourrée en Rondeau
Indy 112

Bourrée II in A Major, KK 1404
Chopin 60

Bourrée in C Minor
Mozart, L. 14

Bread and Butter
Mozart, W. A. (Attr.) 23

By the Campfire, Op. 3/86, No. 6
Kabalevsky 138

Cat on a Swing
Khachaturian 136

Catch Me If You Can!, Op. 55, No. 23
Kirchner 66

Chinese March
Tcherepnin 134

Cossack Dance
Czerný 30

Dance on the Lawn, Op. 27, No. 11
Kabalevsky 88

Dance Song, Sz. 42:49
Bartók 83

Danish Folk Tune, Op. 3, No. 1
Nielsen 118

Divertimento No. I in F Major
Myslivecek 54

Echo in the Mountains, Op. 28, No. 19
Maykapar 78

Ecossaise in G Major
Hässler 21

Fairy Tale Princess, The, Op. 76, No. 8
Friedman 130

Fantasia in G Major, Wq. 117:8
Bach, C.P.E. 94

Gallop Marquis, KKp 1240a
Chopin 61

Gavotte II in D Major, BWV 811, from *English Suite No. 6*
Bach, J. S. 93

German Dance in B-flat Major, D. 783, No. 7
Schubert 59

German Dance in F Major, WoO 42, No. 1
Beethoven 29

Gigue in D Minor from *Suite No. 4*
Handel 46

Grandmother Tells a Ghost Story, Op. 81, No. 3
Kullak 64

Gypsies, Op. 138, No. 19
Heller 104

Gypsy Dance, Hob. IX:28/6
Haydn 20

Happy Birthday, Op. 69, No. 7
Shostakovich 142

Having Fun Crossing Hands
Türk 26

Hopping, Op. 39, No. 18
Kabalevsky 37

In a Quiet Mood
Goedicke 80

Jade Wheel Turns in the Dew, The
Tcherepnin 135

Jigg in A Major
Reinagle 57

Kanzonette in C Major
Neefe 22

Klavierstück in F Major (Piano Piece), K. 33b
   Mozart, W. A. 56

La fille aux cheveux de lin
   (The Girl with the Flaxen Hair), L. 117:8
   Debussy 116

Lame Witch Lurking in the Forest, The, Op. 31, No. 9
   Rebikov 76

Le Lardon—Menuet
   Rameau 43

Little Scherzo, Sz. 52:82
   Bartók 34

March in E-flat Major, BWV Anh. 127,
   from *Anna Magdalena Bach Klavierbüchlein*, 1725
   Bach, J. S. 44

March, Op. 65, No. 10
   Prokofiev 84

Menuett in C Minor
   Handel 16

Menuett in G Major
   Bach, J.C.F. 18

Merry Tune, A, Op. 89, No. 26
   Kabalevsky 38

Minuet in E-flat Major, WoO 10, No. 3
   Beethoven 58

Minuet in G Major
   Bach, W. F. 17

Moderato in C Major
   Bach, J.C.F. 19

Musette in D Major, BWV Anh. 126,
   from *Anna Magdalena Bach Klavierbüchlein*, 1725
   Anonymous 9

Night on the River, Op. 27, No. 4
   Kabalevsky 39

Old Dance, An, Op. 27, No. 7
   Kabalevsky 90

Orientale, Op. 123, No. 9
   Chaminade 70

Parsley and Celery, Sz. 42:21
   Bartók 33

Patriotic Song, Op. 12, No. 8
   Grieg 68

Poetic Valse No. 5
   Granados 77

Poetic Valse No. 6
   Granados 122

Polka
   Wagner 63

Prelude in A Major, Op. 28, No. 7
   Chopin 62

Prelude in C Minor, Op. 28, No. 20
   Chopin 100

Prelude in G Minor, Op. 11, No. 22
   Scriabin 128

Presto in F Major
   Reinagle 25

Russian Menuet
   Shostakovich 41

Skipping
   Khachaturian 36

Soirée Polka
   Foster 106

Solfeggio in C Minor, Wq. 117:2
   Bach, C.P.E. 48

Sonata in G Major, K. 431
   Scarlatti 11

Song of the Lark, Op. 39, No. 22
   Tchaikovsky 110

Song of Youth, Op. 45, No. 1
   Backer-Grøndahl 67

Song without Words, Op. 30, No. 3
   Mendelssohn 96

Sound of the Hunting Horn, The
   Oesten 32

Swineherd's Dance, Sz. 52:77
   Bartók 35

Tambourin in F Major
   Gambarini 47

Tango, The (Endless)
   Satie 119

Tempo Giusto
   Bach, J. C. 52

Those Broken Octaves!
   Türk 27

To a Wild Rose, Op. 51, No. 1
   MacDowell 72

Traümerei (Dreaming), Op. 15, No. 7
   Schumann 98

Valse Viennoise (Viennese Waltz), Op. 32, No. 8
   Schmitt 126

Valsette, Op. 40, No. 1
   Sibelius 74

Vivace in D Major, Hob. I:92/4
   Haydn 50

Waltz in B Minor, D. 145:6
   Schubert 95

Waltz in E Major, Op. 39, No. 2
   Brahms 108

Waltz, Op. 27, No. 1
   Kabalevsky 40

Warlike Song, A, Op. 89, No. 30
   Kabalevsky 91

Who Will Win the Argument?, Op. 88, No. 2
   Kabalevsky 140

Contents Listed by Level

EARLY INTERMEDIATE

Anonymous
Musette in D Major, BWV Anh. 126,
  from *Anna Magdalena Bach Klavierbüchlein*, 1725 9

Bach, Johann Christoph Friedrich
Menuett in G Major 18
Moderato in C Major 19

Bach, Johann Sebastian
Aria in D Minor, BWV 515,
  from *Anna Magdalena Bach Klavierbüchlein*, 1725 10

Bach, Wilhelm Friedemann
Minuet in G Major 17

Bartók, Béla
Little Scherzo, Sz. 52:82 34
Parsley and Celery, Sz. 42:21 33
Swineherd's Dance, Sz. 52:77 35

Beethoven, Ludwig van
Bagatelle in A Major, Op. 119, No. 10 ...28
German Dance in F Major, WoO 42, No. 1 ...29

Czerný, Joseph
Cossack Dance 30

Handel, George Frideric
Menuett in C Minor 16

Hässler, Johann Wilhelm
Ecossaise in G Major 21

Haydn, Franz Joseph
Gypsy Dance, Hob. IX:28/6 20

Kabalevsky, Dmitri
Hopping, Op. 39, No. 18 37
Merry Tune, A, Op. 89, No. 26 38
Night on the River, Op. 27, No. 4 ...39
Waltz, Op. 27, No. 1 40

Khachaturian, Aram
Skipping 36

Mozart, Leopold
Bourrée in C Minor 14

Mozart, Wolfgang Amadeus (Attr.)
Bread and Butter 23

Neefe, Christian Gottlob
Kanzonette in C Major 22

Oesten, Theodore
Sound of the Hunting Horn, The 32

Reinagle, Alexander
Allegro in B-flat Major 24
Presto in F Major 25

Scarlatti, Domenico
Aria in D Minor, K. 32 12
Sonata in G Major, K. 431 11

Shostakovich, Dmitri
Russian Menuet 41

Türk, Daniel Gottlob
Having Fun Crossing Hands 26
Those Broken Octaves! 27

Weber, Carl Maria von
Ballett in F Major 31

INTERMEDIATE

Bach, Carl Philipp Emanuel
Solfeggio in C Minor, Wq. 117:2 48

Bach, Johann Christian
Tempo Giusto 52

Bach, Johann Sebastian
March in E-flat Major, BWV Anh. 127,
  from *Anna Magdalena Bach Klavierbüchlein*, 1725 44

Backer-Grøndahl, Agathe
Song of Youth, Op. 45, No. 1 67

Bartók, Béla
Above the Tree, Under the Tree, Sz. 42:45 ...82
Dance Song, Sz. 42:49 83

Beethoven, Ludwig van
Minuet in E-flat Major, WoO 10, No. 3 ...58

Chaminade, Cécile
Orientale, Op. 123, No. 9 70

Chopin, Frédéric
Bourrée II in A Major, KK 1404 60
Gallop Marquis, KKp 1240a 61
Prelude in A Major, Op. 28, No. 7 ...62

Gambarini, Elisabetta de
Tambourin in F Major 47

Goedicke, Alexander
In a Quiet Mood 80

Granados, Enrique
Poetic Valse No. 5 77

Grieg, Edvard
Patriotic Song, Op. 12, No. 8 68

Handel, George Frideric
Gigue in D Minor from *Suite No. 4* 46

Haydn, Franz Joseph
Vivace in D Major, Hob. I:92/4 50

Kabalevsky, Dmitri
Dance on the Lawn, Op. 27, No. 11 88
Old Dance, An, Op. 27, No. 7 90
Warlike Song, A, Op. 89, No. 30 91

Kirchner, Theodor
Catch Me If You Can!, Op. 55, No. 23 66

Khachaturian, Aram
Bedtime Story 86

Kullak, Theodor
Grandmother Tells a Ghost Story, Op. 81, No. 3 64

MacDowell, Edward
To a Wild Rose, Op. 51, No. 1 72

Maykapar, Samuel
Echo in the Mountains, Op. 28, No. 19 78

Mozart, Wolfgang Amadeus
Klavierstück in F Major (Piano Piece), K. 33b 56

Myslivecek, Josef
Divertimento No. I in F Major 54

Prokofiev, Sergei
March, Op. 65, No. 10 84

Rameau, Jean-Philippe
Le Lardon—Menuet 43

Rebikov, Vladimir
Lame Witch Lurking in the Forest, The,
Op. 31, No. 9 76

Reinagle, Alexander
Jigg in A Major 57

Schubert, Franz
German Dance in B-flat Major, D. 783, No. 7 59

Sibelius, Jean
Valsette, Op. 40, No. 1 74

Wagner, Richard
Polka 63

LATE INTERMEDIATE

Bach, Carl Philipp Emanuel
Fantasia in G Major, Wq. 117:8 94

Bach, Johann Sebastian
Gavotte II in D Major, BWV 811,
from *English Suite No. 6* 93

Brahms, Johannes
Waltz in E Major, Op. 39, No. 2 108

Chopin, Frédéric
Prelude in C Minor, Op. 28, No. 20 100

Debussy, Claude
Album Leaf, L. 133 114
La fille aux cheveux de lin
(The Girl with the Flaxen Hair), L. 117:8 116

Foster, Stephen C.
Soirée Polka 106

Friedman, Ignacy
Fairy Tale Princess, The, Op. 76, No. 8 130

Granados, Enrique
Bell of the Afternoon, The, from *Bocetos* 120
Poetic Valse No. 6 122

Gurlitt, Cornelius
Bolero 102

Heller, Stephen
Gypsies, Op. 138, No. 19 104

Indy, Vincent d'
Bourrée en Rondeau 112

Kabalevsky, Dmitri
By the Campfire, Op. 3/86, No. 6 138
Who Will Win the Argument?, Op. 88, No. 2 140

Khachaturian, Aram
Cat on a Swing 136

Liszt, Franz
Bell Tolls, The, S. 238 101

Maykapar, Samuel
Blacksmith, The, Op. 8, No. 5 124

Mendelssohn, Felix
Song without Words, Op. 30, No. 3 96

Nielsen, Carl
Danish Folk Tune, Op. 3, No. 1 118

Satie, Erik
Tango, The (Endless) 119

Schmitt, Florent
Valse Viennoise (Viennese Waltz),
Op. 32, No. 8 126

Schubert, Franz
Waltz in B Minor, D. 145:6 95

Schumann, Robert
Traümerei (Dreaming), Op. 15, No. 7 98

Scriabin, Alexander
Prelude in G Minor, Op. 11, No. 22 128

Shostakovich, Dmitri
Happy Birthday, Op. 69, No. 7 142

Tchaikovsky, Peter Ilyich
Song of the Lark, Op. 39, No. 22 110

Tcherepnin, Alexander
Bagatelle, Op. 5, No. 1 132
Chinese March 134
Jade Wheel Turns in the Dew, The 135

Early Intermediate

Musette in D Major
from *Anna Magdalena Bach Klavierbüchlein*, 1725

Anonymous
BWV Anh. 126

(a) Dynamics and articulation are editorial.

Aria in D Minor
from *Anna Magdalena Bach Klavierbüchlein*, 1725

Johann Sebastian Bach (1685–1750)
BWV 515

ⓐ Dynamics and articulation are editorial.

Sonata in G Major

Domenico Scarlatti (1685–1757)
K. 431

(a) Dynamics and articulation are editorial.   (b)

Aria in D Minor

Domenico Scarlatti (1685–1757)
K. 32

ⓐ Dynamics and articulation are editorial.

Bourrée in C Minor

Leopold Mozart
(1719–1787)

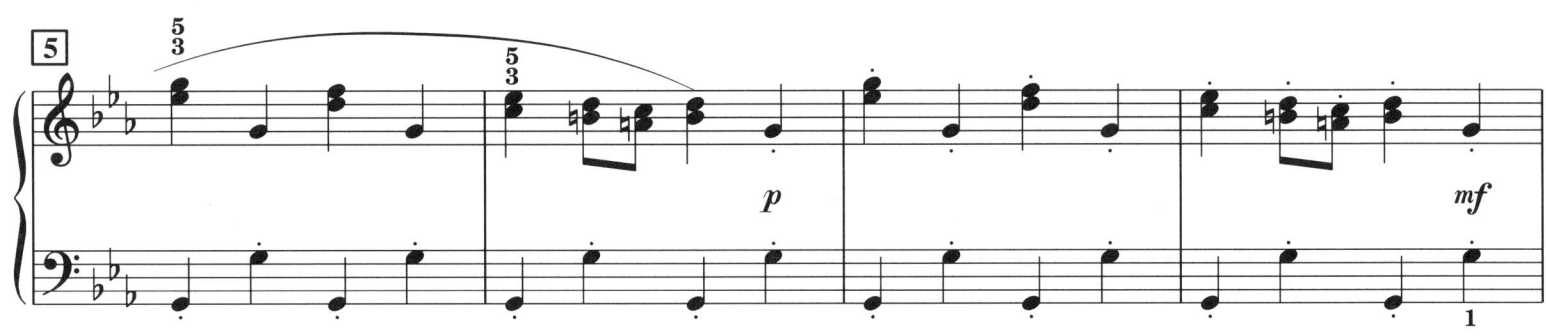
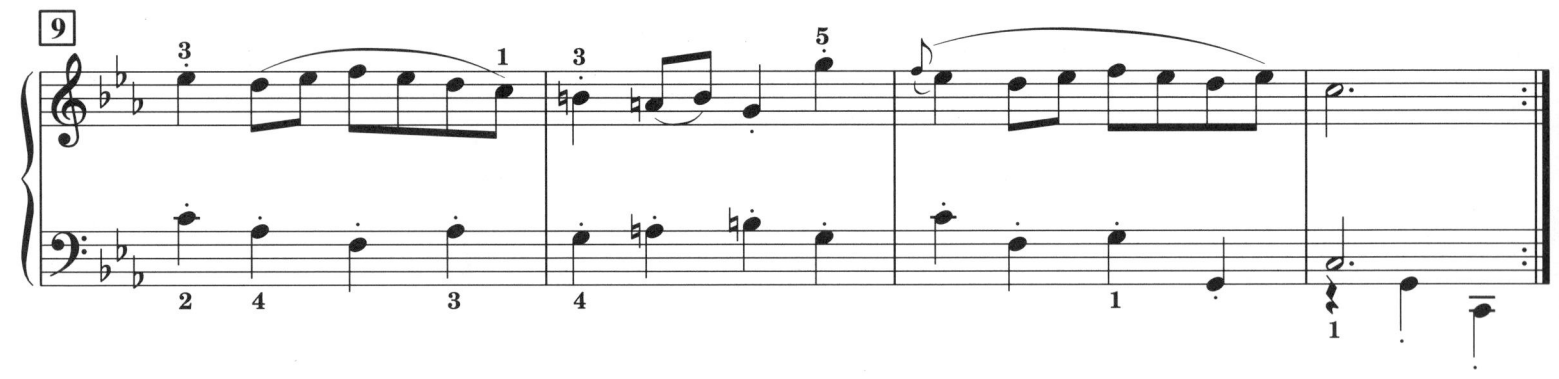
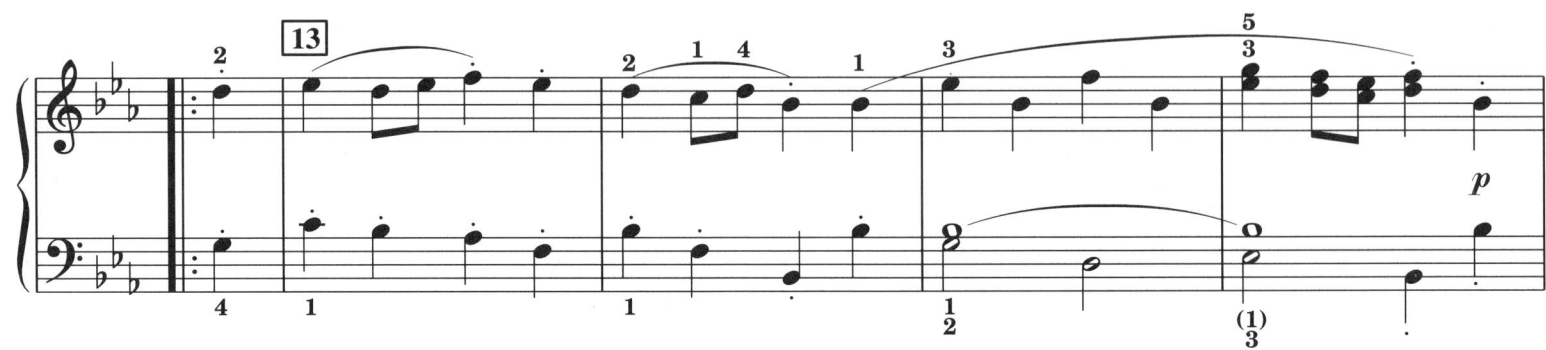

ⓐ Articulation is editorial.   ⓑ

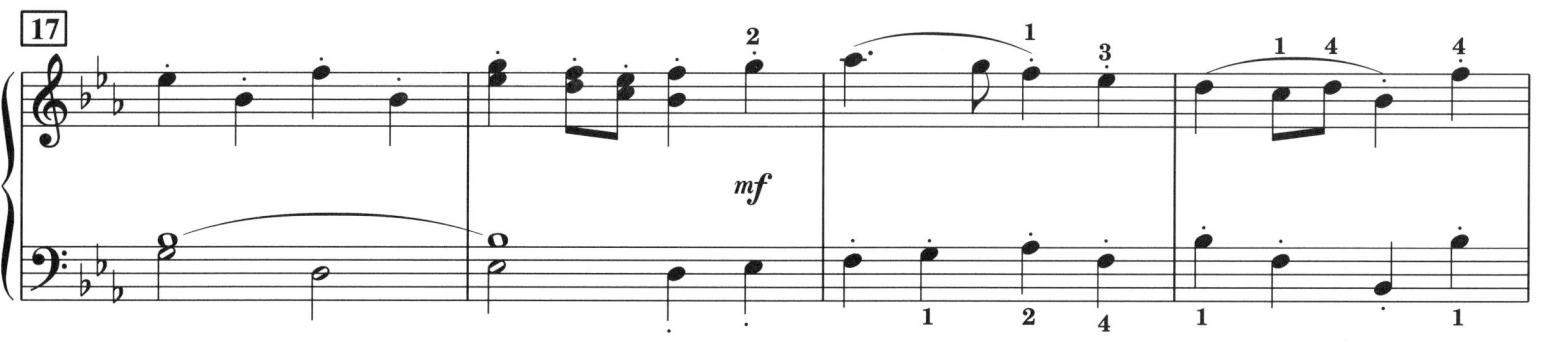
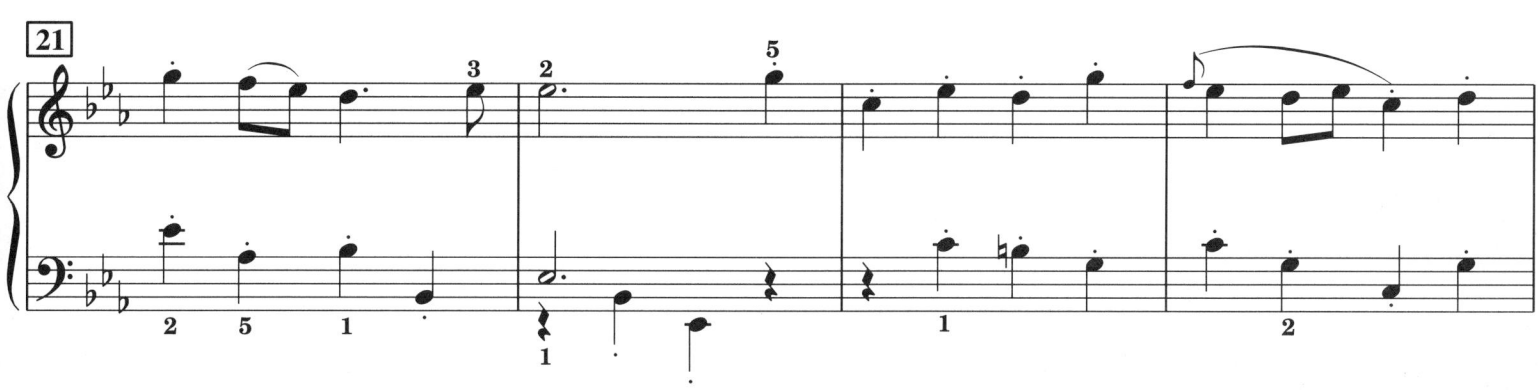
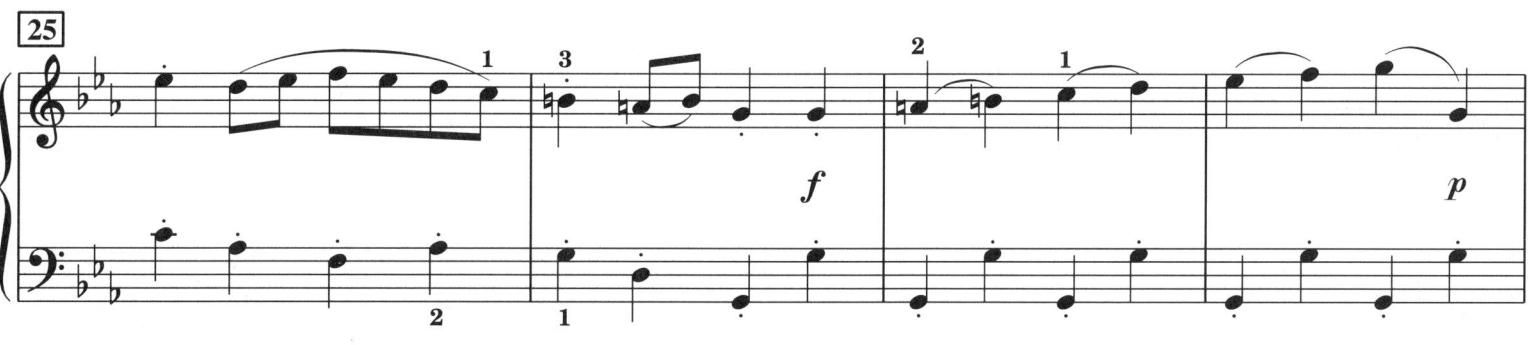
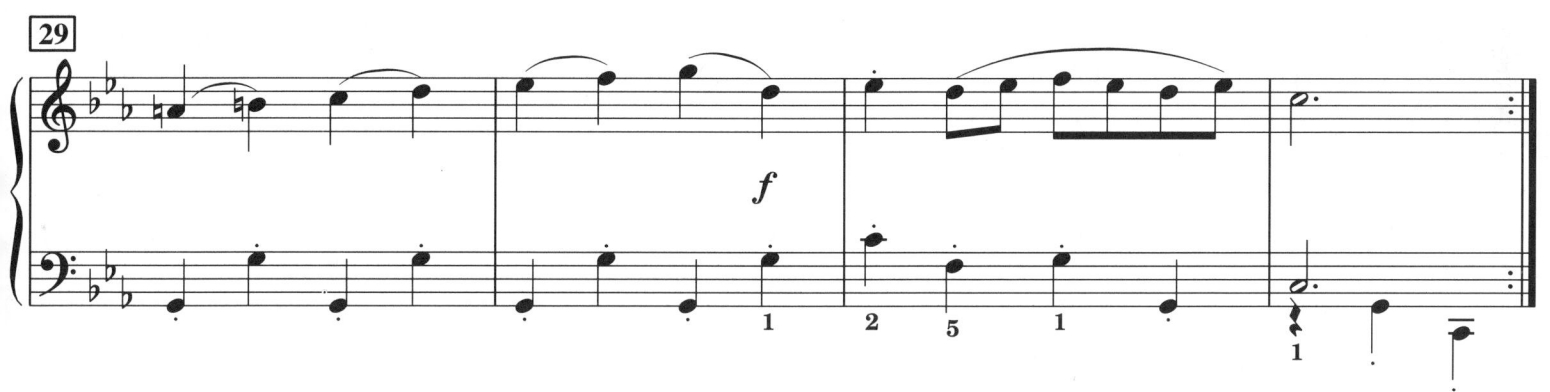

Menuett in C Minor

George Frideric Handel
(1685–1759)

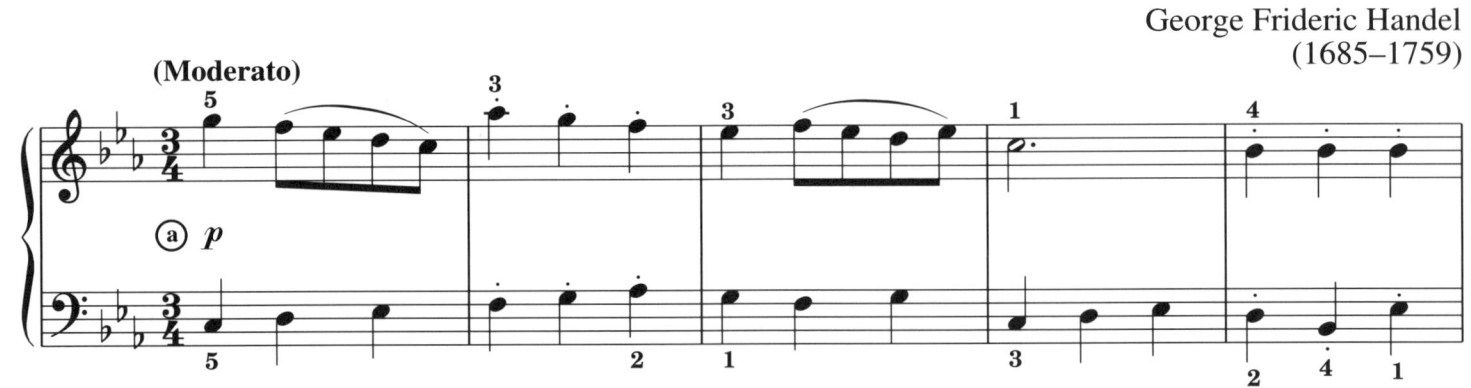

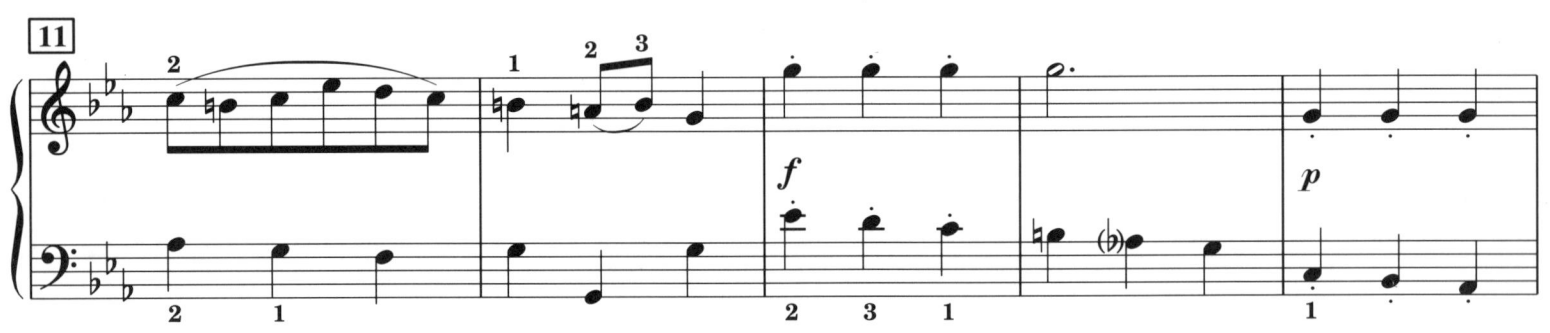

ⓐ Dynamics and articulation are editorial.

Minuet in G Major

Wilhelm Friedemann Bach
(1710–1784)

ⓐ Dynamics and articulation are editorial.

Menuett in G Major

Johann Christoph Friedrich Bach
(1732–1795)

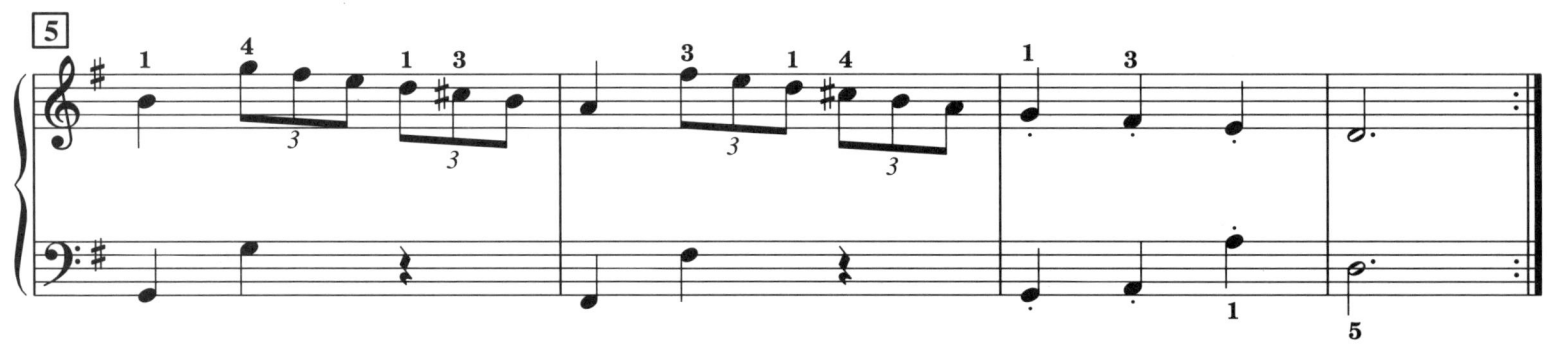

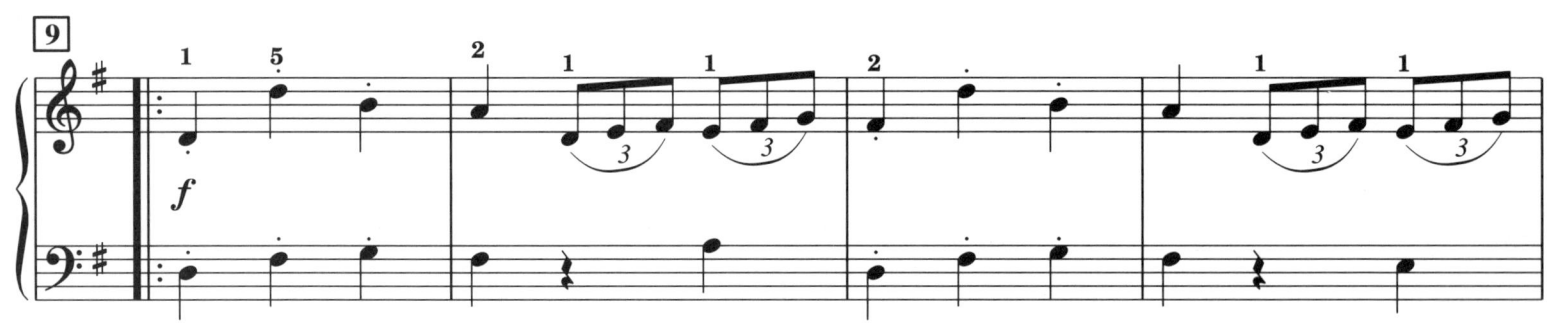

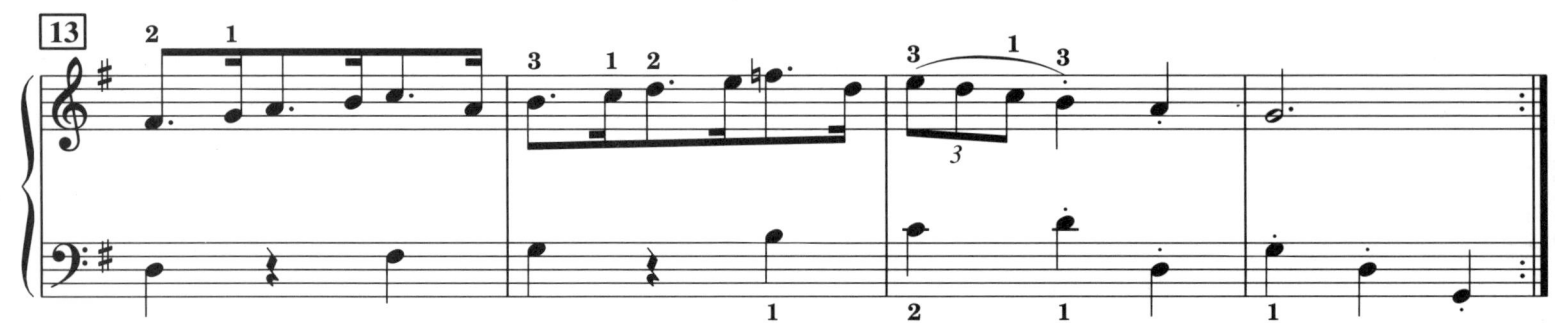

(a) Dynamics and articulation are editorial.

Moderato in C Major (a)

Johann Christoph Friedrich Bach
(1732–1795)

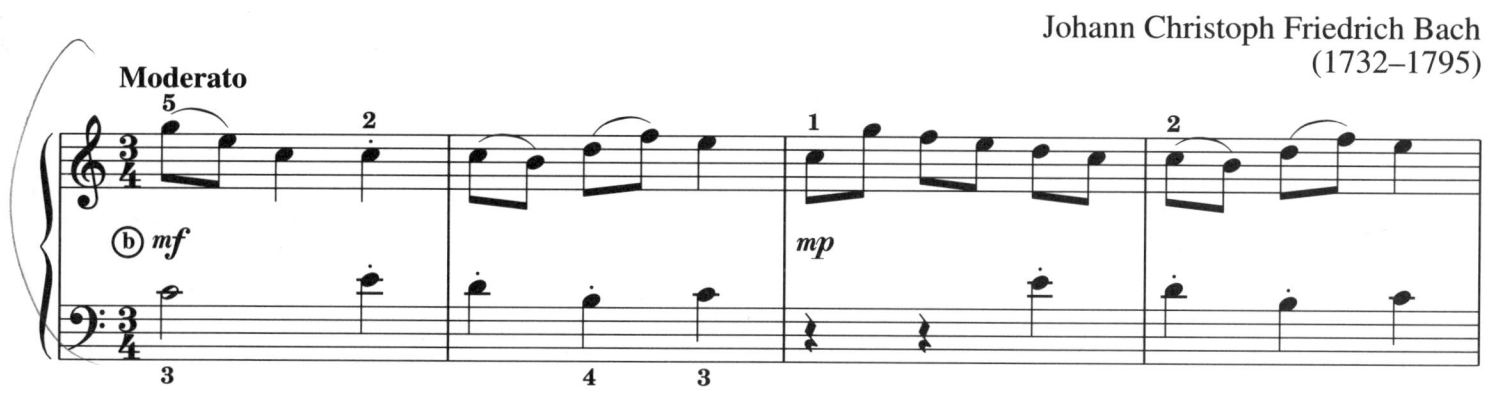
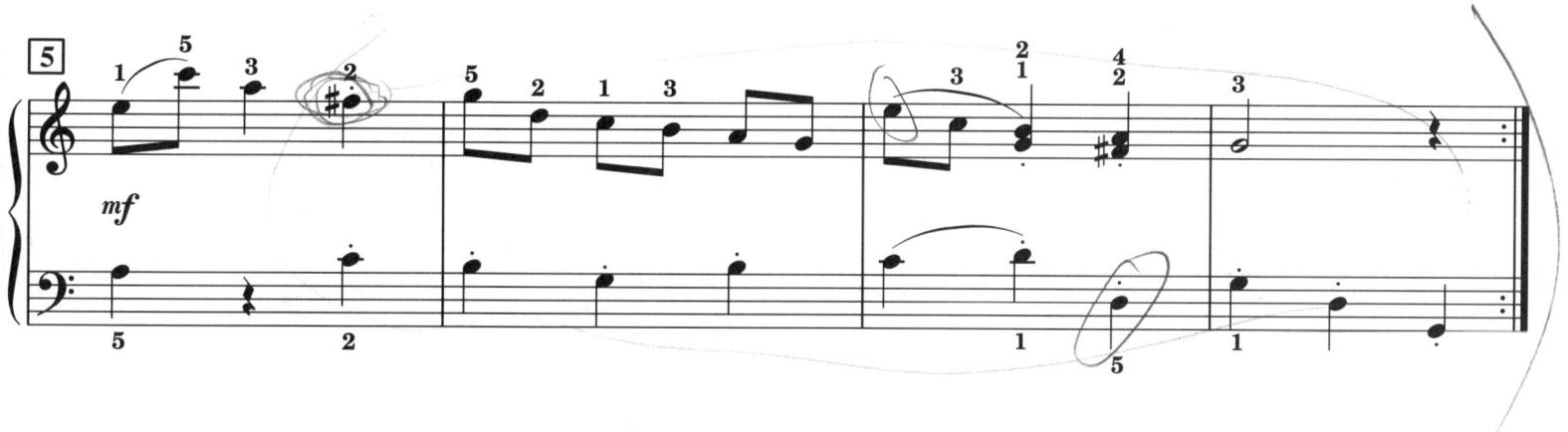
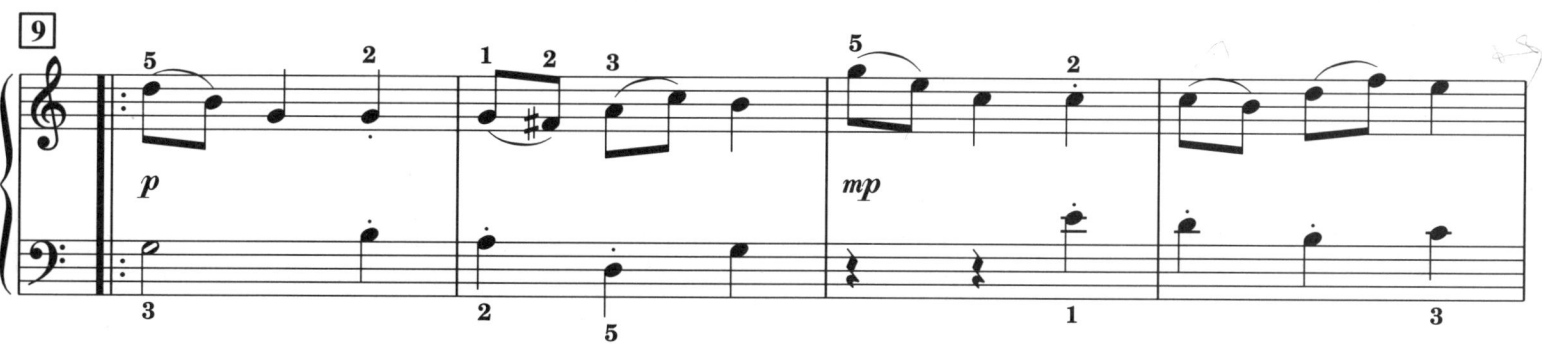
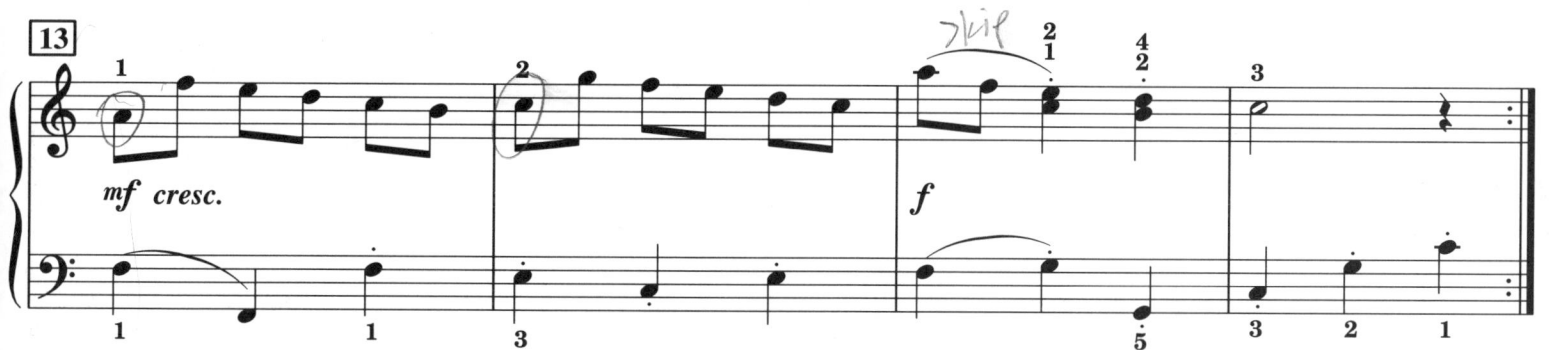

(a) Title is editorial; original was untitled.
(b) Dynamics and articulation are editorial.

Gypsy Dance

Franz Joseph Haydn (1732–1809)
Hob. IX:28/6

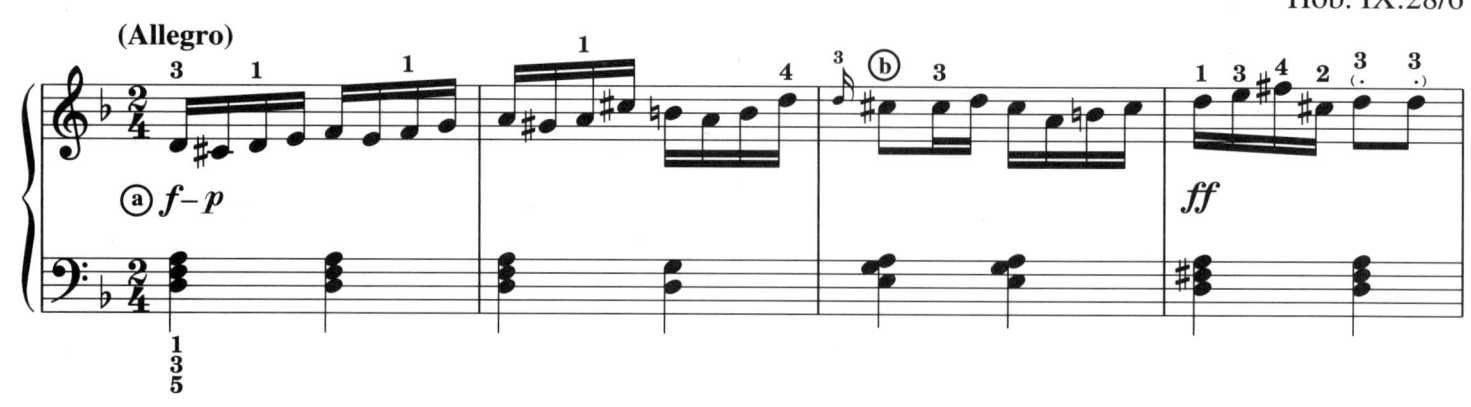

ⓐ Dynamics are editorial.

Ecossaise in G Major

Johann Wilhelm Hässler
(1747–1822)

(a) Dynamics and articulation are editorial.

Kanzonette in C Major

Christian Gottlob Neefe
(1748–1798)

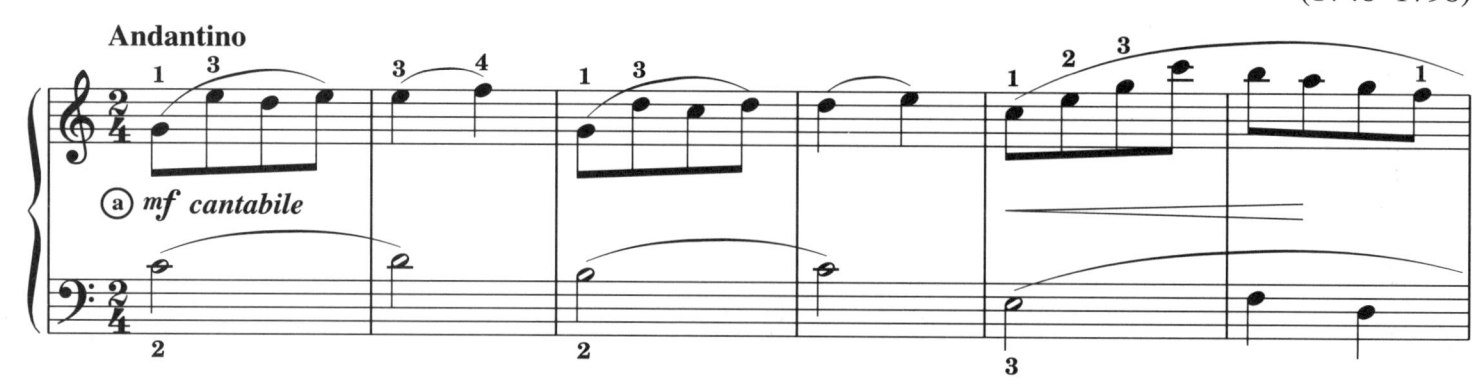
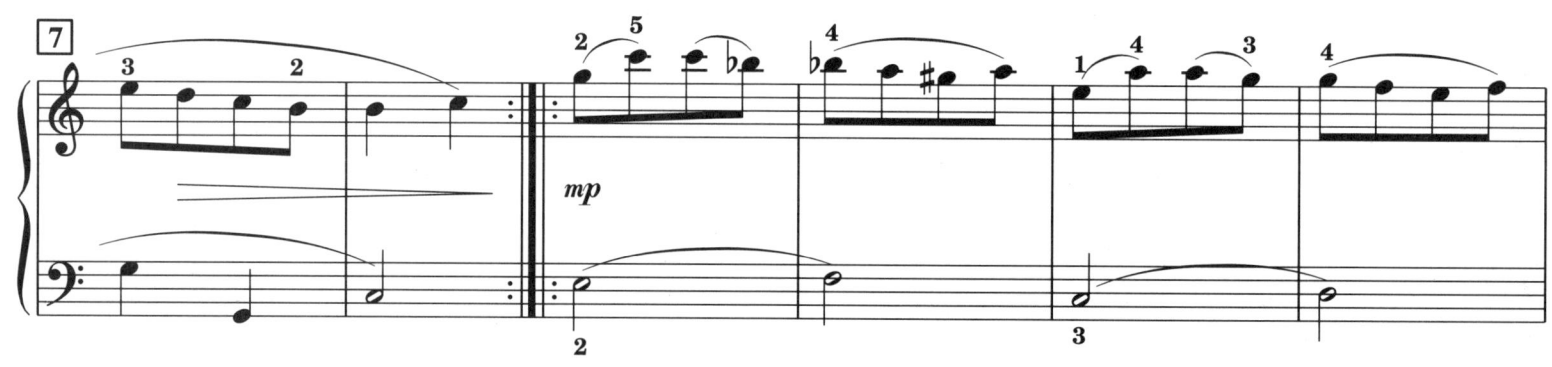
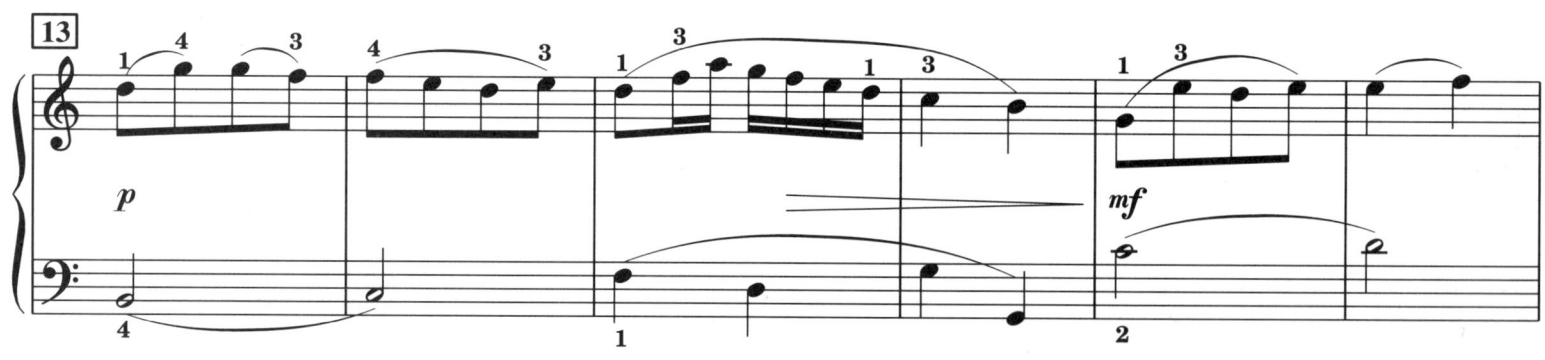

ⓐ Dynamics and articulation are editorial.

Bread and Butter

Attributed to
Wolfgang Amadeus Mozart
(1756–1791)

ⓐ Dynamics and articulation are editorial.

Allegro in B-flat Major

Alexander Reinagle
(1756–1809)

Presto in F Major

Alexander Reinagle
(1756–1809)

ⓐ Dynamics are editorial.

Having Fun Crossing Hands

Daniel Gottlob Türk
(1756–1813)

(a) Articulation is editorial.

Those Broken Octaves!

Daniel Gottlob Türk
(1756–1813)

Bagatelle in A Major

(Joyfully)
Allegramente

Ludwig van Beethoven (1770–1827)
Op. 119, No. 10

(a) Dynamics are editorial.

German Dance in F Major

Ludwig van Beethoven (1770–1827)
WoO 42, No. 1

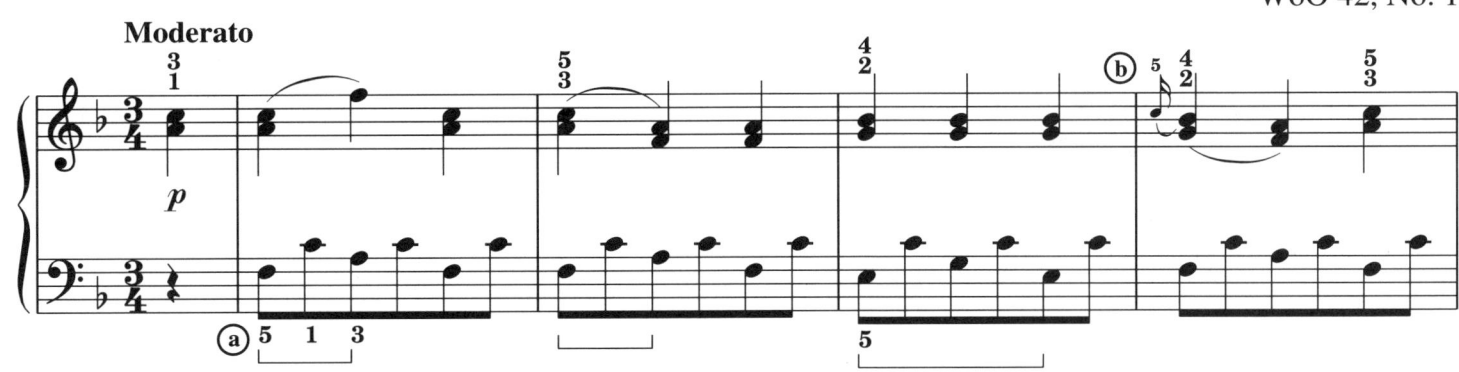

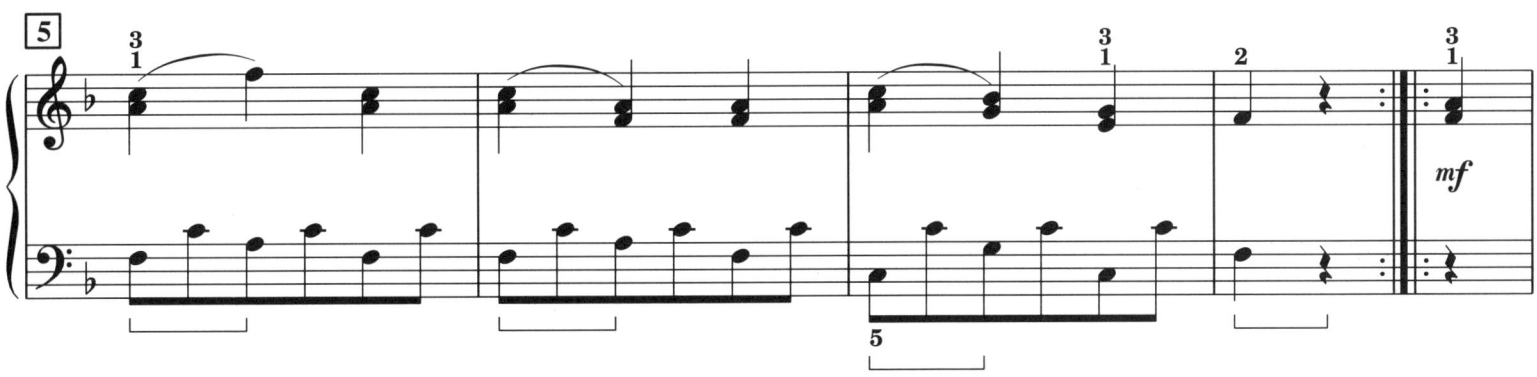

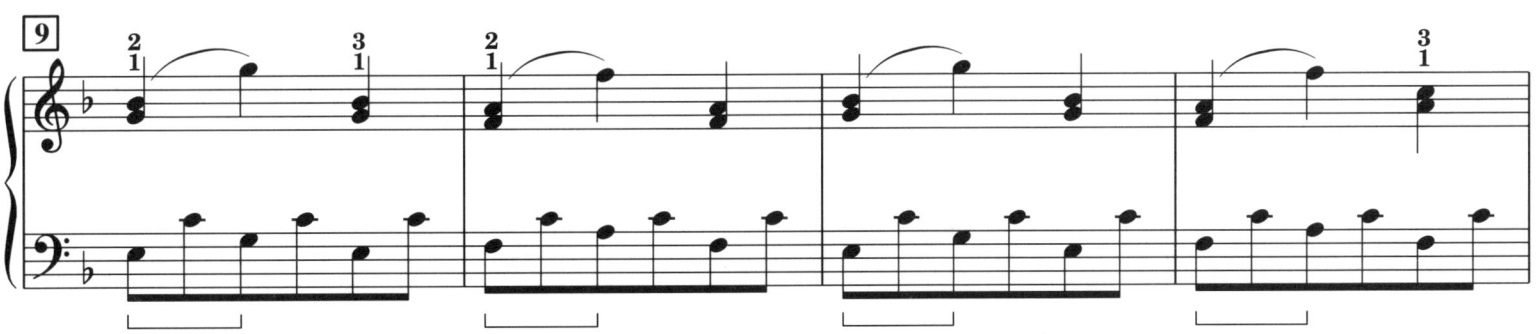

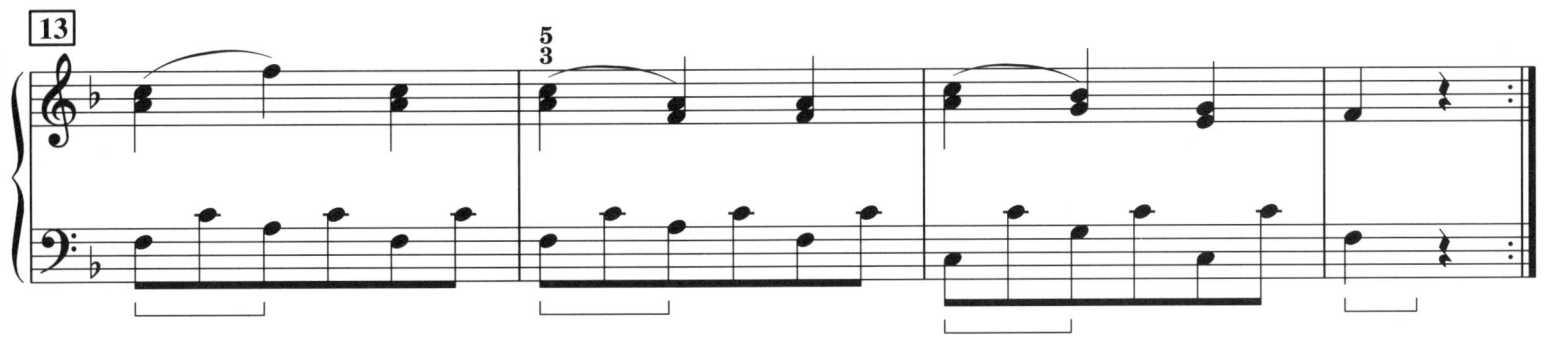

ⓐ Pedal indications are editorial.
ⓑ Play the grace notes on the beat.

Cossack Dance

Joseph Czerný
(1785–1842)

ⓐ Articulation is editorial.
ⓑ Play the grace notes on the beat in measures 2–4, 6–7, 18–20 and 21–22.

Ballett in F Major

Carl Maria von Weber
(1786–1826)

ⓐ Play grace notes before the beat in measures 1, 2 and 18.

The Sound of the Hunting Horn

Theodore Oesten
(1813–1870)

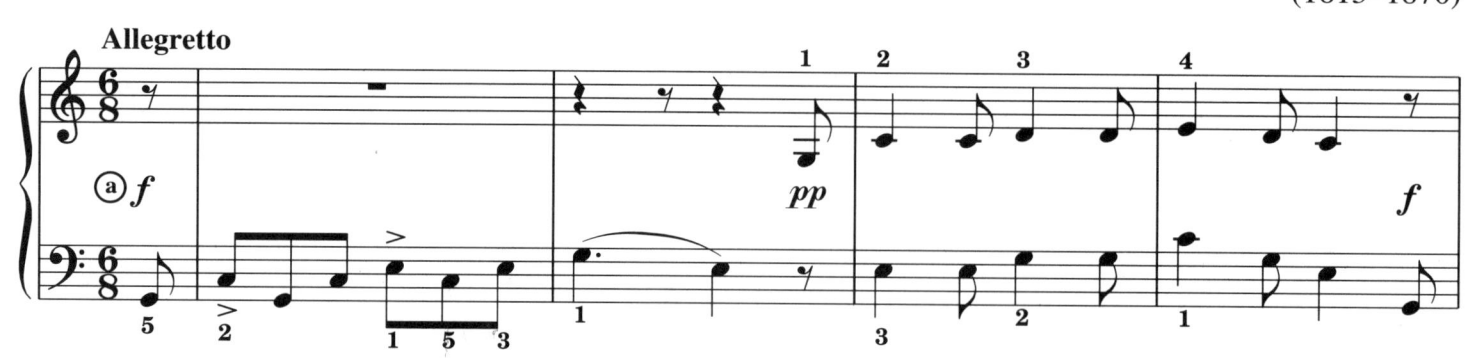
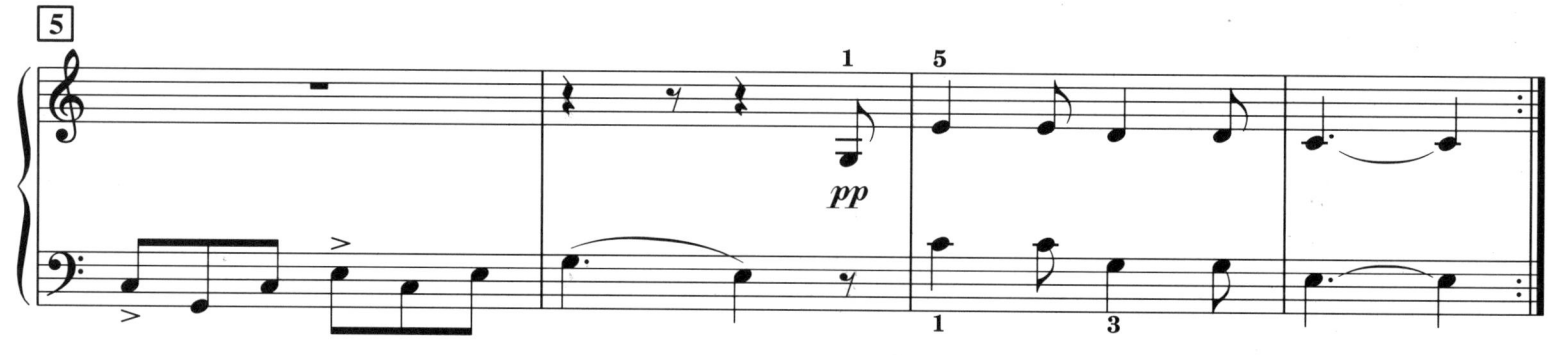

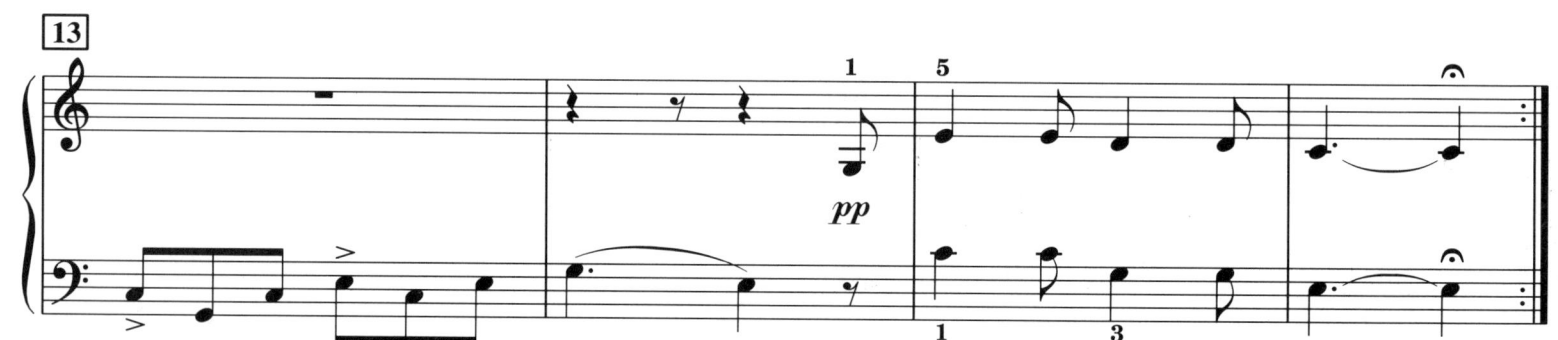

ⓐ Dynamics are editorial.

Parsley and Celery

Béla Bartók (1881–1945)
Sz. 42:21

ⓐ Metronome marking is Bartók's.

Little Scherzo

Béla Bartók (1881–1945)
Sz. 52:82

ⓐ Metronome marking is Bartók's.

Swineherd's Dance

Béla Bartók (1881–1945)
Sz. 52:77

(a) Metronome marking is Bartók's.

Skipping

Aram Khachaturian
(1903–1978)

Hopping

Dmitri Kabalevsky (1904–1987)
Op. 39, No. 18

A Merry Tune

Dmitri Kabalevsky (1904–1987)
Op. 89, No. 26

Night on the River

Dmitri Kabalevsky (1904–1987)
Op. 27, No. 4

ⓐ Pedal indications are editorial.

Waltz

Dmitri Kabalevsky (1904–1987)
Op. 27, No. 1

(a) Pedal indications are editorial.

Russian Menuet (a)

Dmitri Shostakovich
(1906–1975)

(a) Original title was *Menuet*.
(b) Play the grace notes before the beat in measures 2, 6, 9, 11, 13, 15, 18 and 22.
(c) Pedal indications are editorial.

Intermediate

Le Lardon (a)
Menuet

Jean-Philippe Rameau
(1683–1764)

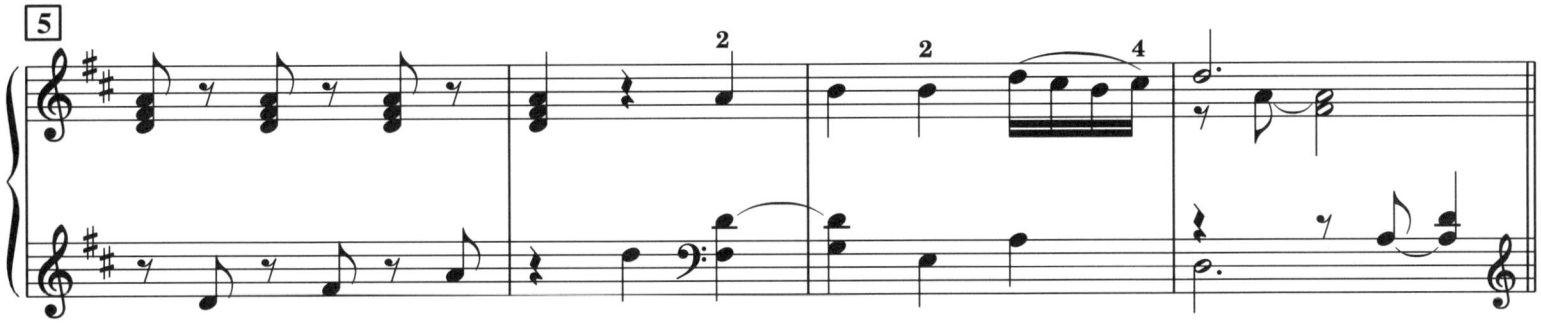

(a) "Lardon" refers to a process whereby meat is cut into strips and lard placed between the strips. Rameau may be drawing a humorous parallel with the fingers of the left hand (lard) playing between the right hand (meat).

(b) Dynamics and articulation are editorial.

March in E-flat Major
from *Anna Magdalena Bach Klavierbüchlein*, 1725

Johann Sebastian Bach (1685–1750)
BWV Anh. 127

ⓐ Dynamics and articulation are editorial.　ⓑ

Gigue in D Minor
from *Suite No. 4*

George Frideric Handel
(1685–1759)

ⓐ Dynamics are editorial.

Tambourin in F Major

Elisabetta de Gambarini
(1731–1765)

(a) Dynamics and articulation are editorial.

Solfeggio in C Minor

Carl Philipp Emanuel Bach (1714–1788)
Wq. 117:2

(a) A *solfeggio* is properly a vocal study and is not often used with instrumental music.
(b) Pedal indications are editorial.

Vivace in D Major

Franz Joseph Haydn (1732–1809)
Hob. I:92/4

ⓐ Dynamics and articulation are editorial.

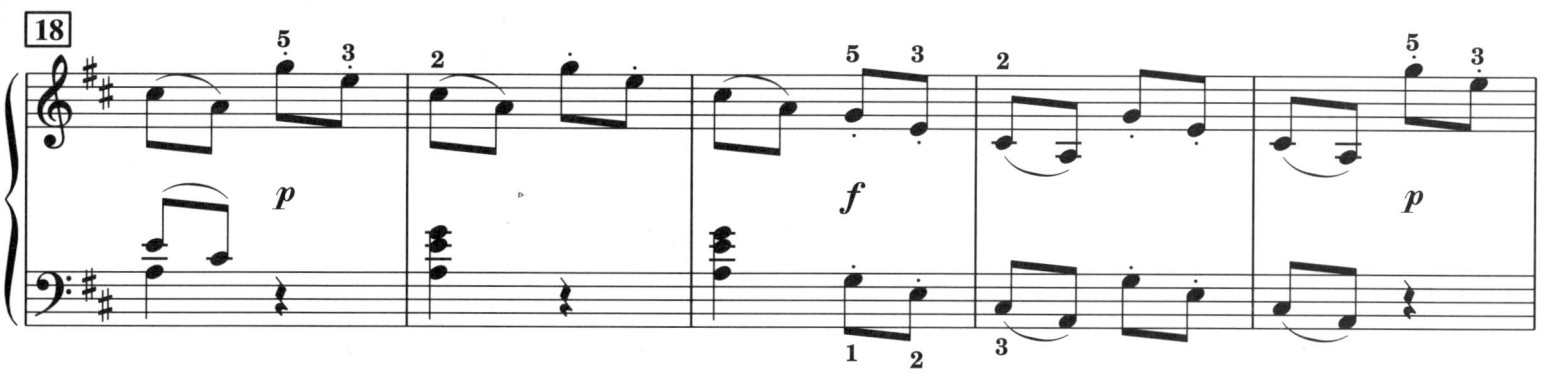

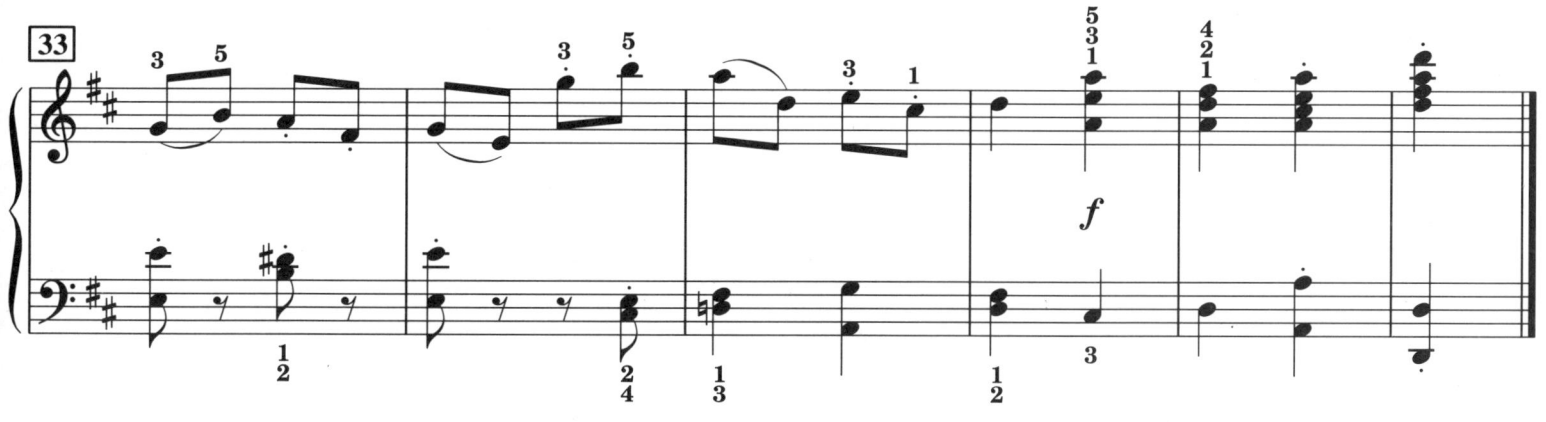

Tempo Giusto

Johann Christian Bach
(1735–1782)

ⓐ Dynamics and articulation are editorial.

Divertimento No. I in F Major

Josef Myslivecek
(1738–1781)

ⓐ Articulation is editorial.

Klavierstück in F Major
(Piano Piece)

Wolfgang Amadeus Mozart (1756–1791)
K. 33b

ⓐ Dynamics and articulation are editorial.

Jigg in A Major

Alexander Reinagle
(1756–1809)

Minuet in E-flat Major

Ludwig van Beethoven (1770–1827)
WoO 10, No. 3

(a) Articulation and pedal indications are editorial.
(b) Play the grace notes on the beat in measures 18 and 20.

German Dance in B-flat Major

Franz Schubert (1797–1828)
D. 783, No. 7

(a) Pedal indications are editorial.

Bourrée II in A Major

Frédéric Chopin (1810–1849)
KK 1404

ⓐ Dynamics, articulation and pedal indications are editorial.
ⓒ The final A in the second ending is editorial.

Gallop Marquis[a]

Frédéric Chopin (1810–1849)
KKp 1240a

[a] Chopin's friend George Sand had two pet dogs, Marquis and Dib. Their lively dances may have inspired Chopin to write this piece.
[b] Dynamics, phrasing and pedal indications are editorial.

Prelude in A Major

Frédéric Chopin (1810–1849)
Op. 28, No. 7

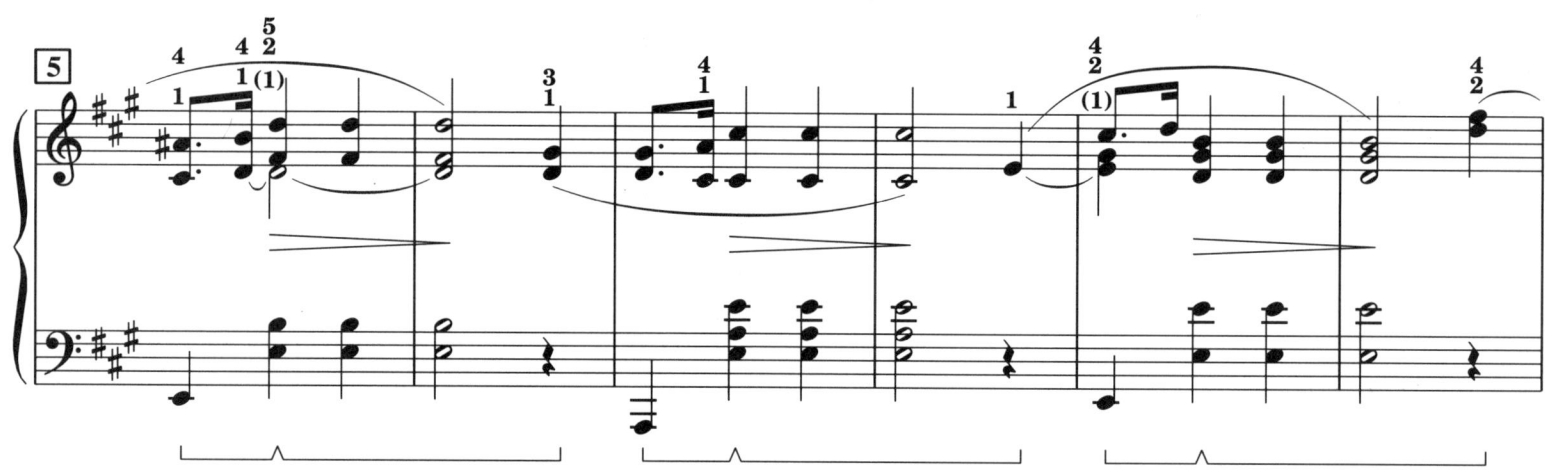
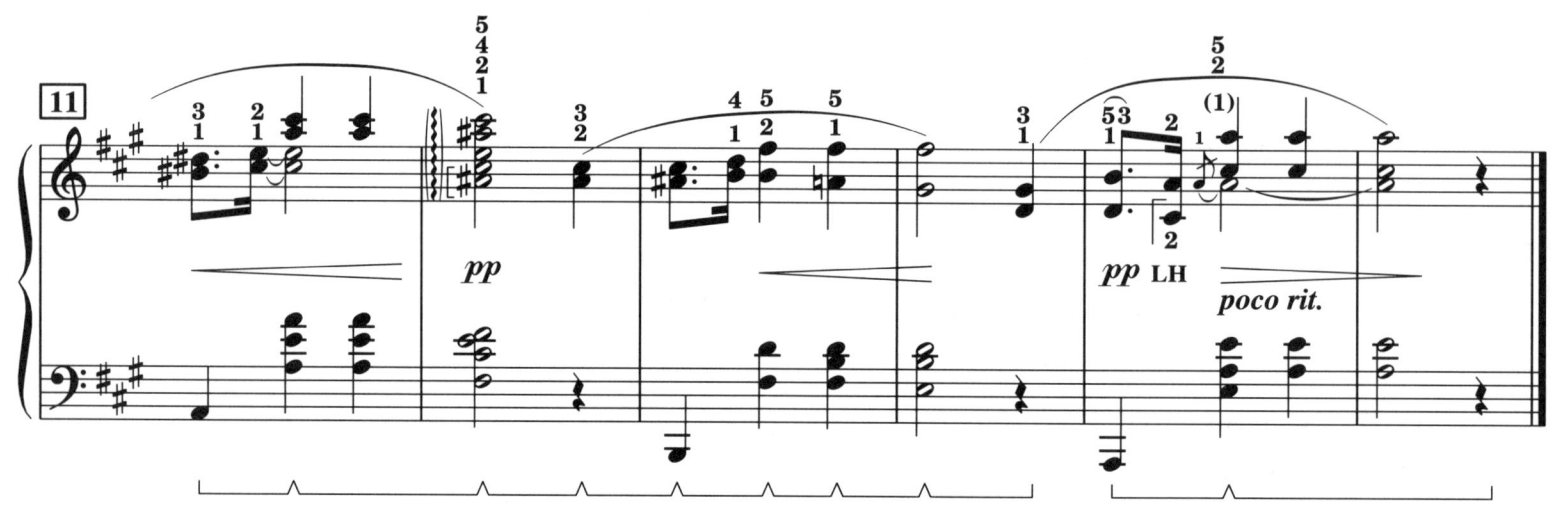

(a) Pedal indications are editorial.

Polka

Richard Wagner
(1813–1883)

(a) Pedal indications are editorial.

Grandmother Tells a Ghost Story

Theodor Kullak (1818–1882)
Op. 81, No. 3

Catch Me If You Can!

Theodor Kirchner (1823–1903)
Op. 55, No. 23

Song of Youth

Agathe Backer-Grøndahl (1847–1907)
Op. 45, No. 1

(a) Pedal indications are editorial.

67

Patriotic Song

Edvard Grieg (1843–1907)
Op. 12, No. 8

Orientale

Cécile Chaminade (1857–1944)
Op. 123, No. 9

ⓐ Pedal indications are editorial.

To a Wild Rose

Edward MacDowell (1860–1908)
Op. 51, No. 1

(a) Pedal indications are editorial.

Valsette

Jean Sibelius (1865–1957)
Op. 40, No. 1

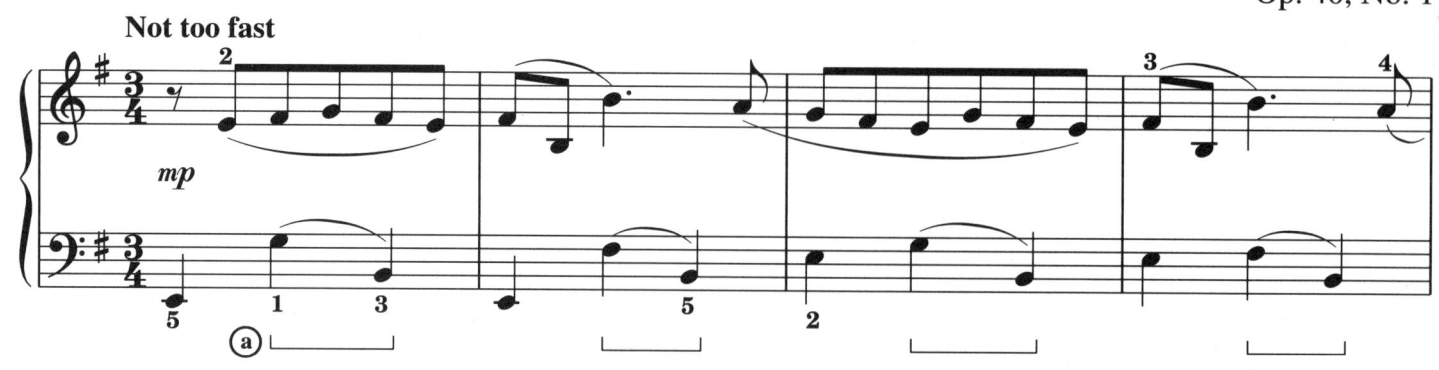

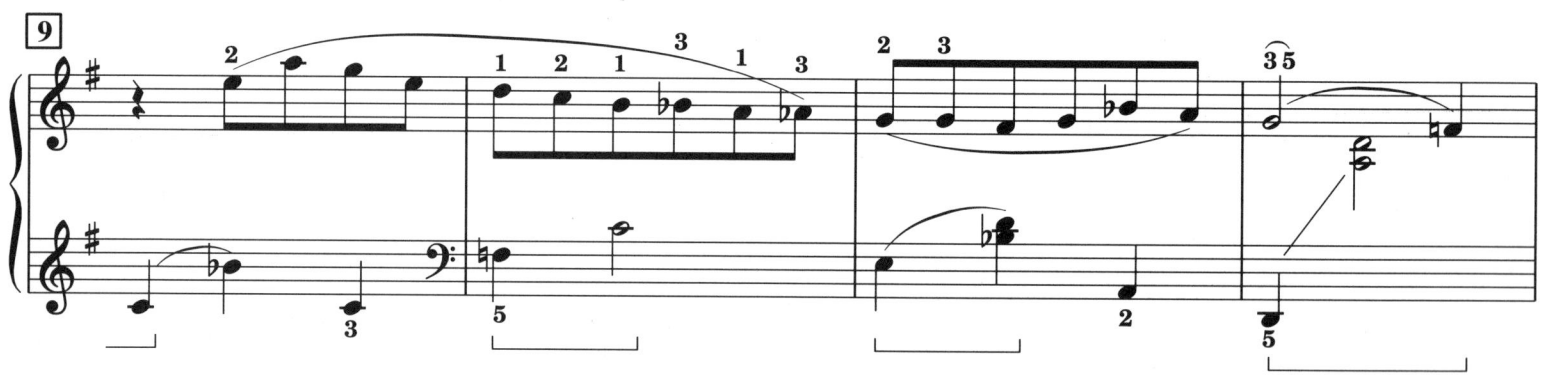
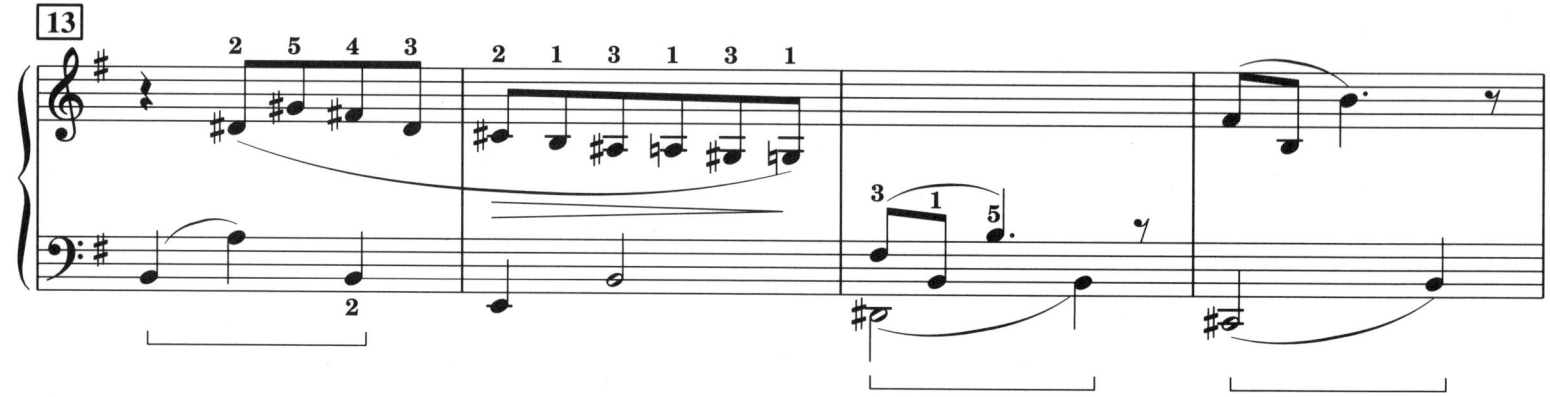

ⓐ Pedal indications are editorial.

(b) Play the grace notes before the beat in measures 27–28.

The Lame Witch Lurking in the Forest

Vladimir Rebikov (1866–1916)
Op. 31, No. 9

Poetic Valse No. 5

Enrique Granados
(1867–1916)

Echo in the Mountains

Samuel Maykapar (1867–1938)
Op. 28, No. 19

ⓐ Dynamics are editorial.

In a Quiet Mood

Alexander Goedicke
(1877–1957)

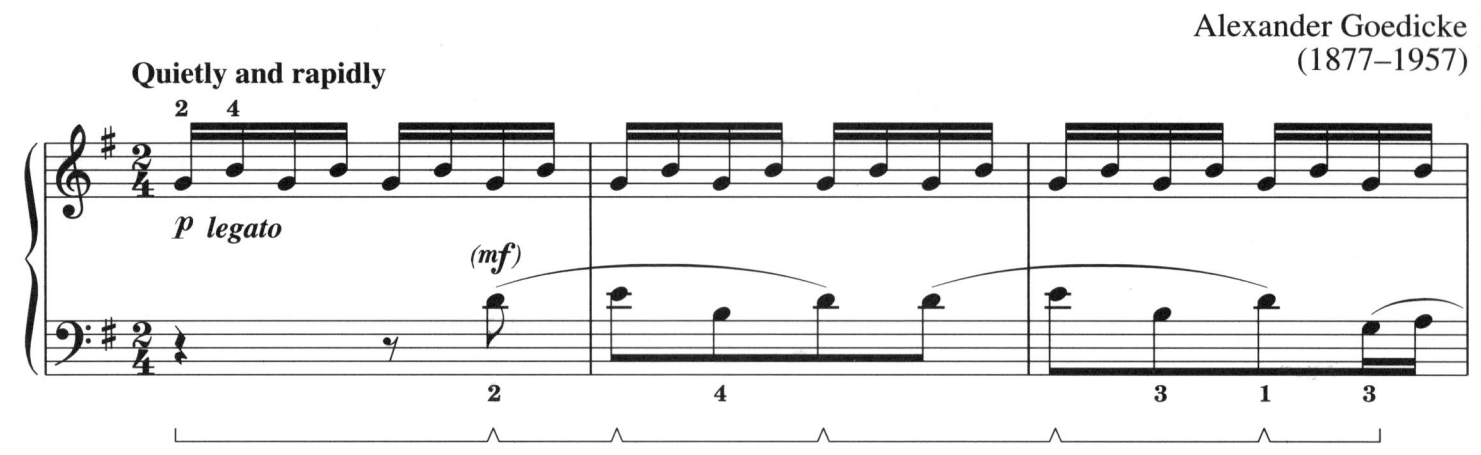
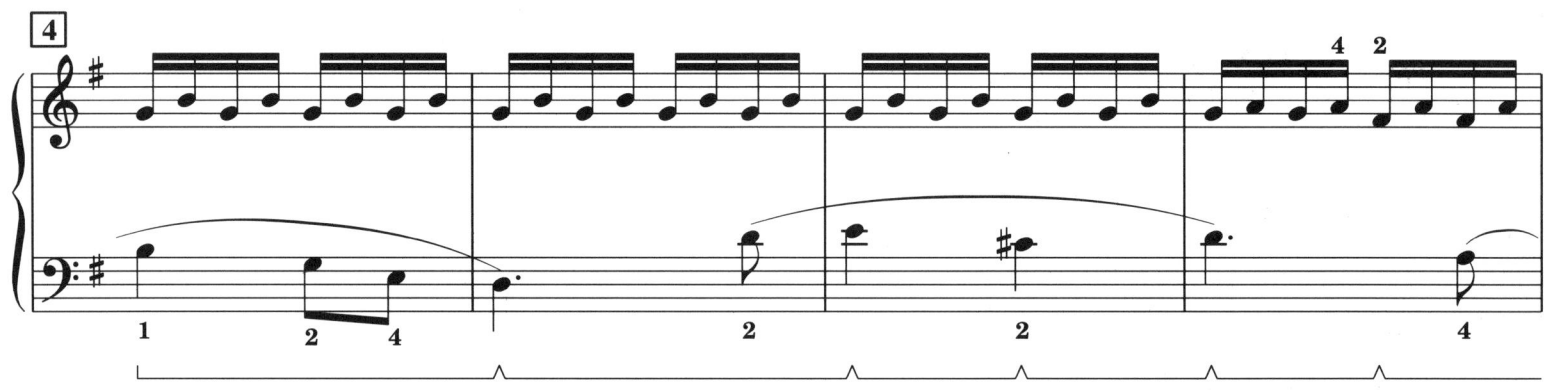
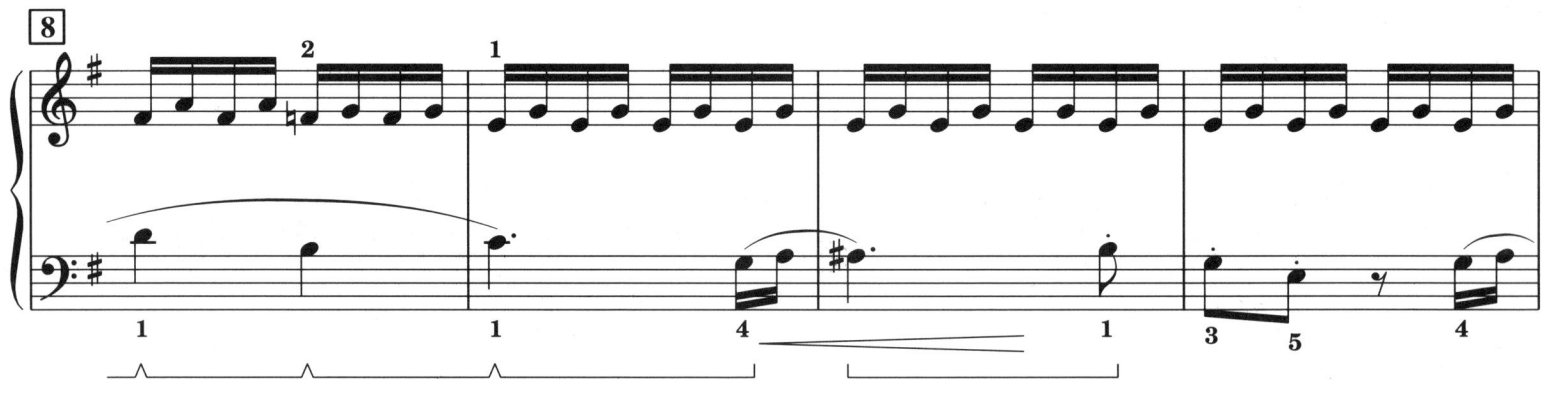
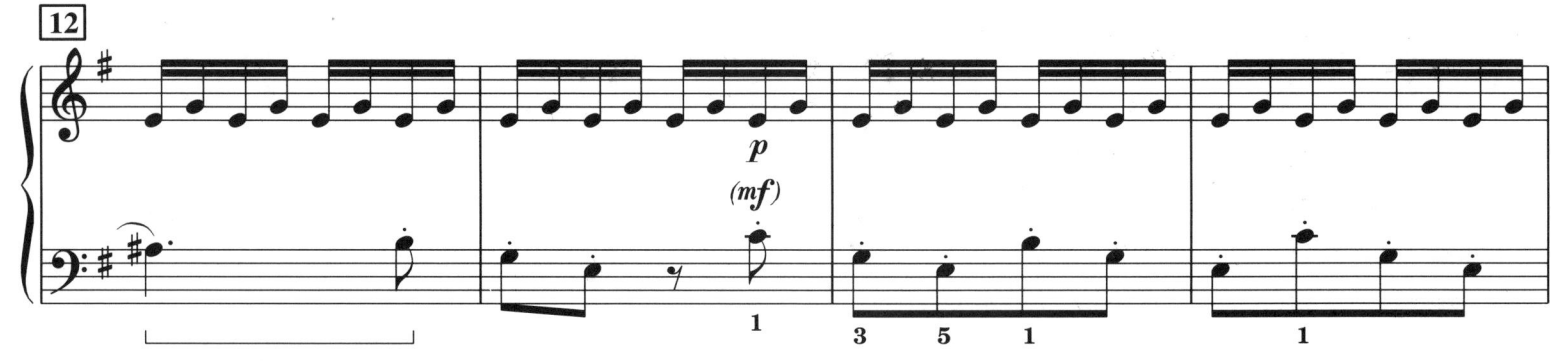

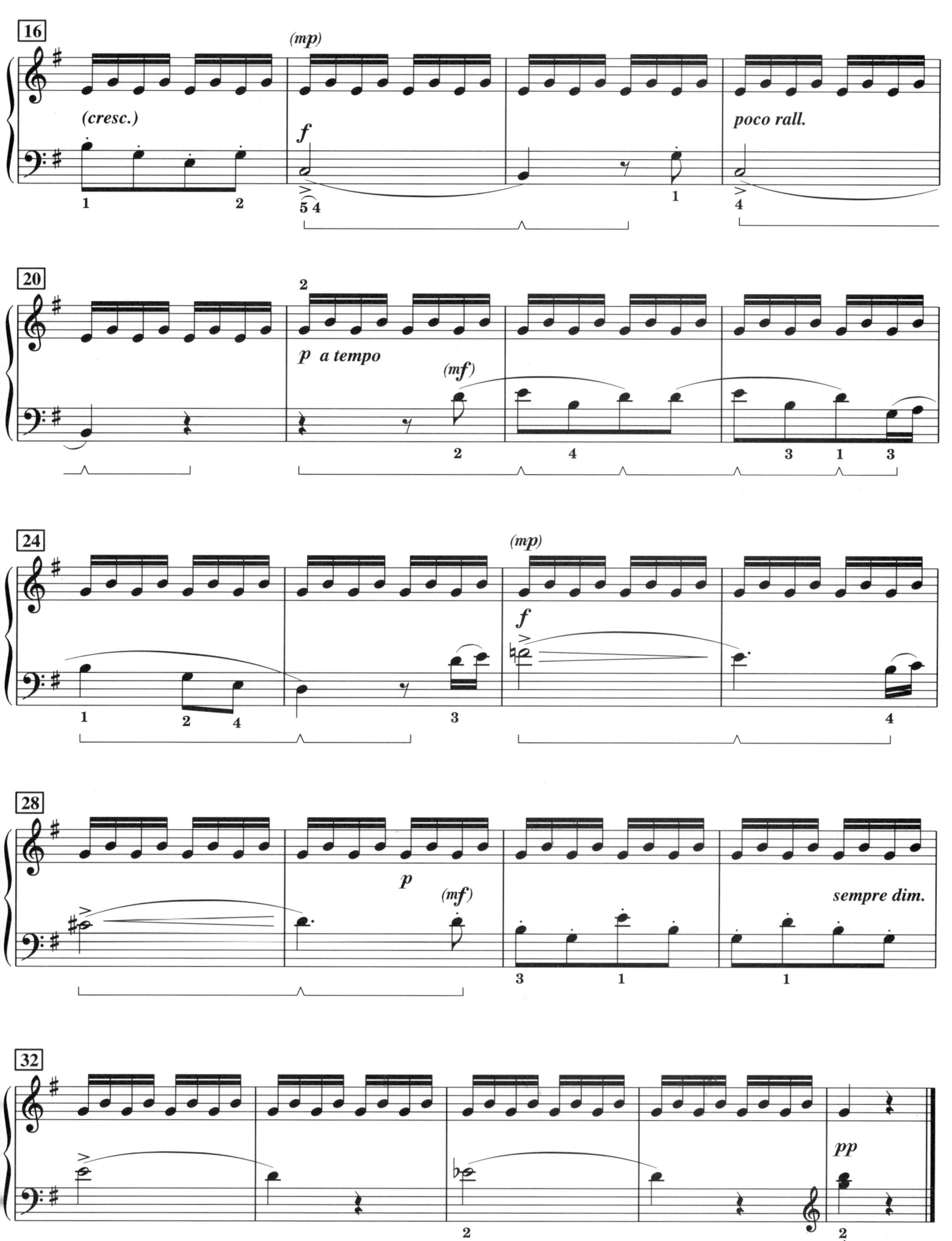

Above the Tree, Under the Tree

Béla Bartók (1881–1945)
Sz. 42:45

Dance Song

Béla Bartók (1881–1945)
Sz. 42:49

March

Sergei Prokofiev (1891–1953)
Op. 65, No. 10

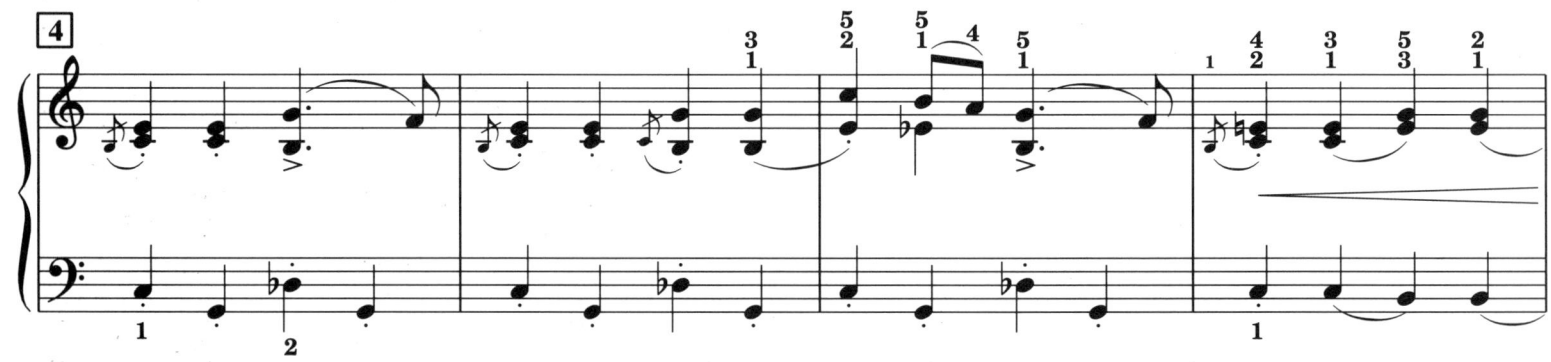

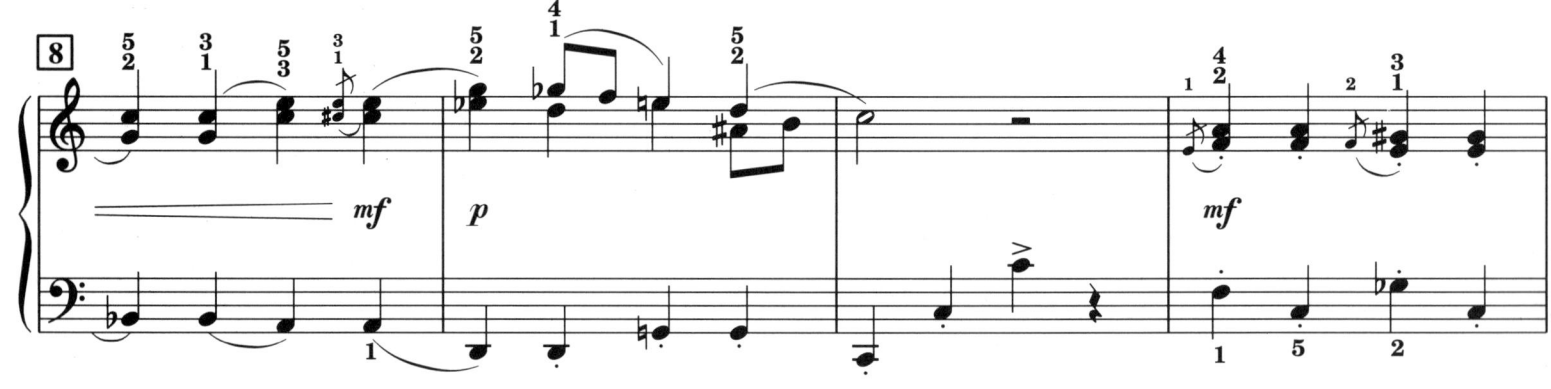

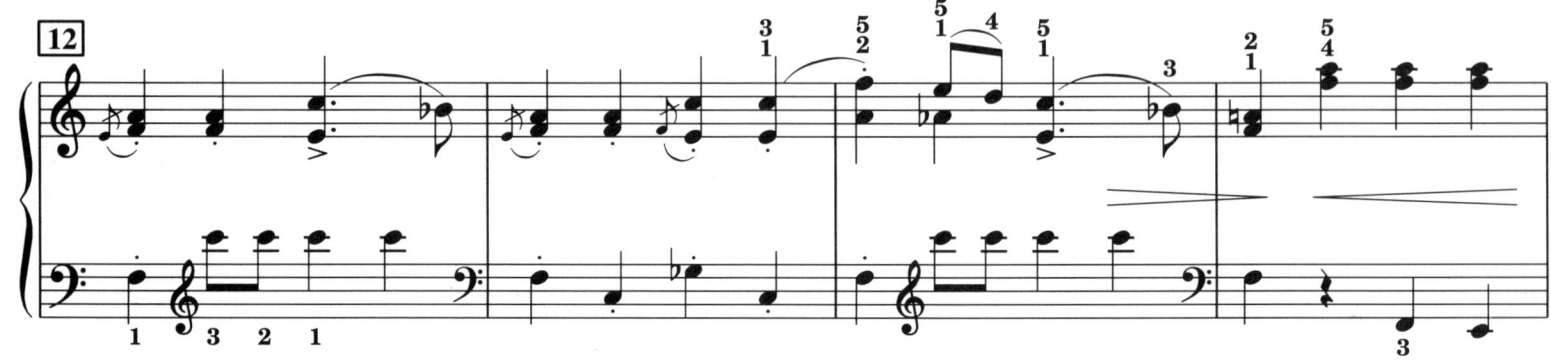

ⓐ Play the grace notes before the beat throughout the piece.

Bedtime Story

Aram Khachaturian
(1903–1978)

Dance on the Lawn

Dmitri Kabalevsky (1904–1987)
Op. 27, No. 11

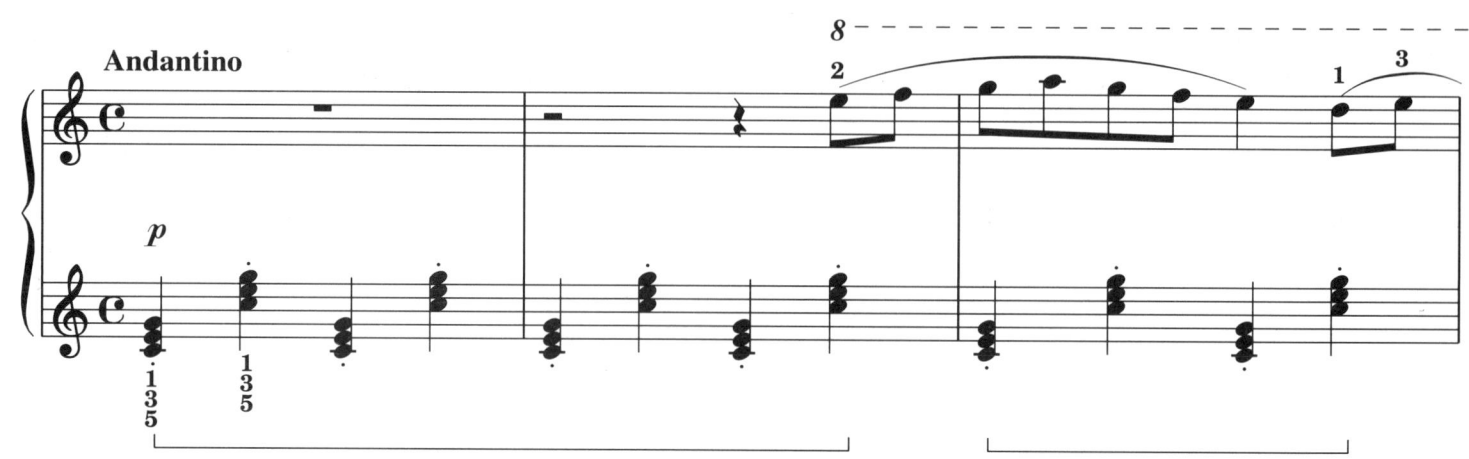
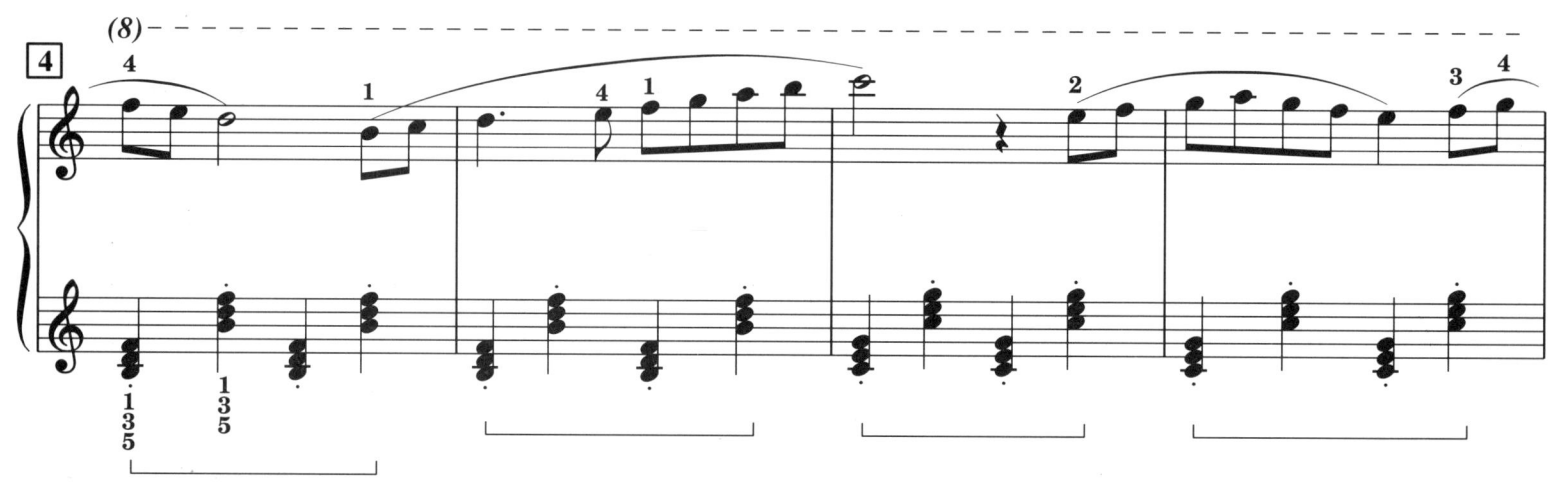
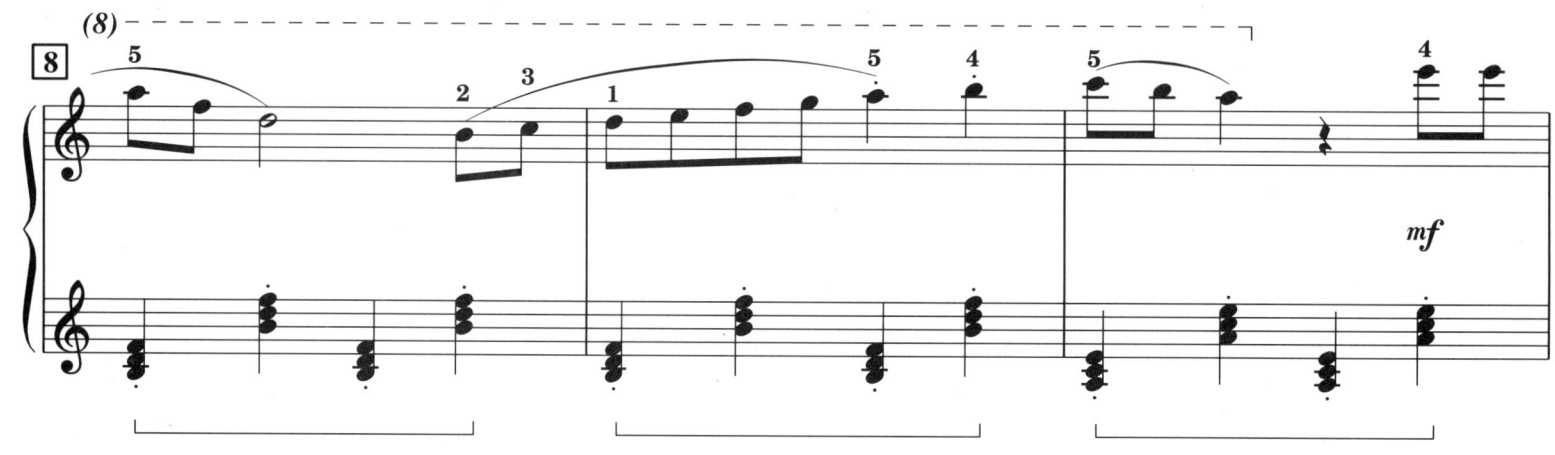

An Old Dance

ⓐ Articulation and pedal indications are editorial.

A Warlike Song

Dmitri Kabalevsky (1904–1987)
Op. 89, No. 30

Late Intermediate

Gavotte II in D Major
from *English Suite No. 6*

Johann Sebastian Bach (1685–1750)
BWV 811

ⓐ Dynamics are editorial.

Fantasia in G Major

Carl Philipp Emanuel Bach (1714–1788)
Wq. 117:8

a) Pedal indications are editorial.

Waltz in B Minor

Franz Schubert (1797–1828)
D. 145:6

ⓐ Pedal indications are editorial.

Song without Words

Felix Mendelssohn (1809–1847)
Op. 30, No. 3

(a) Pedal indications are editorial.

Traümerei
(Dreaming)

Robert Schumann (1810–1856)
Op. 15, No. 7

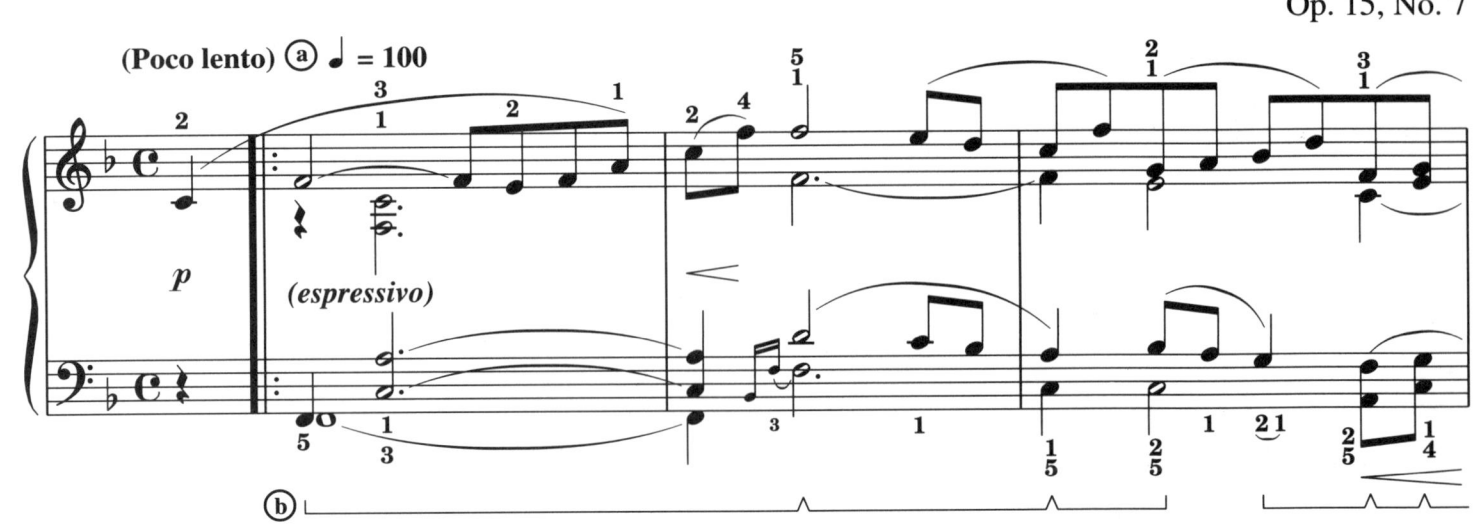

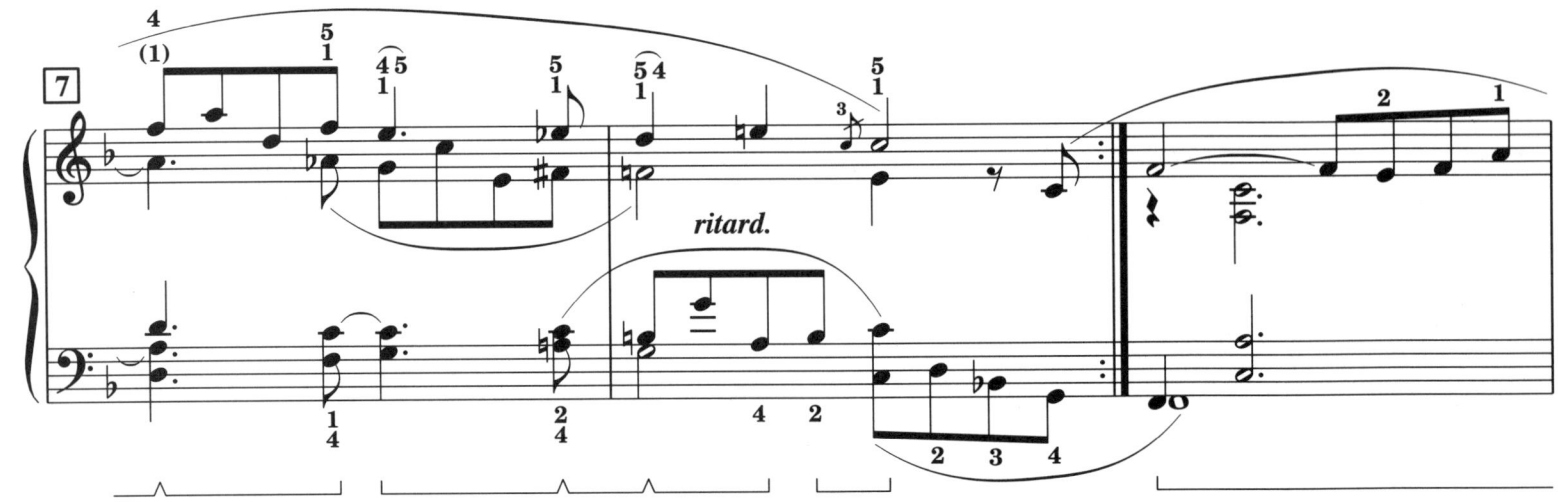

ⓐ Metronome marking is Schumann's.
ⓑ Schumann left pedal marks for measures 1, 13, 16 and 22. All other pedal indications are editorial.

c Play the grace note slowly before the beat to sound almost like an eighth note.

Prelude in C Minor

Frédéric Chopin (1810–1849)
Op. 28, No. 20

(a) Pedal indications are editorial.

The Bell Tolls

Franz Liszt (1811–1886)
S. 238

(a) Pedal indications are editorial.

Bolero

Cornelius Gurlitt
(1820–1901)

ⓐ Pedal indications are editorial.

Gypsies

Stephen Heller (1813–1888)
Op. 138, No. 19

(a) Pedal indications are editorial.
(b) Play the grace notes on the beat throughout the piece.

Soirée Polka

Stephen C. Foster
(1826–1864)

(a) Pedal indications are editorial.

Waltz in E Major

Johannes Brahms (1833–1897)
Op. 39, No. 2

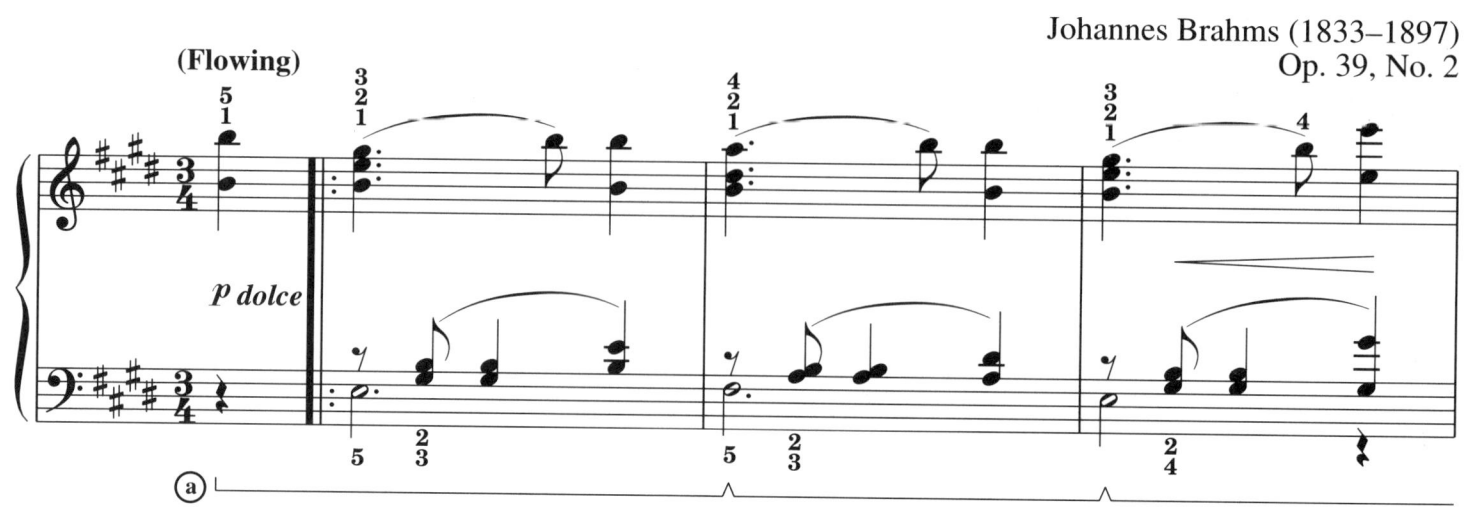

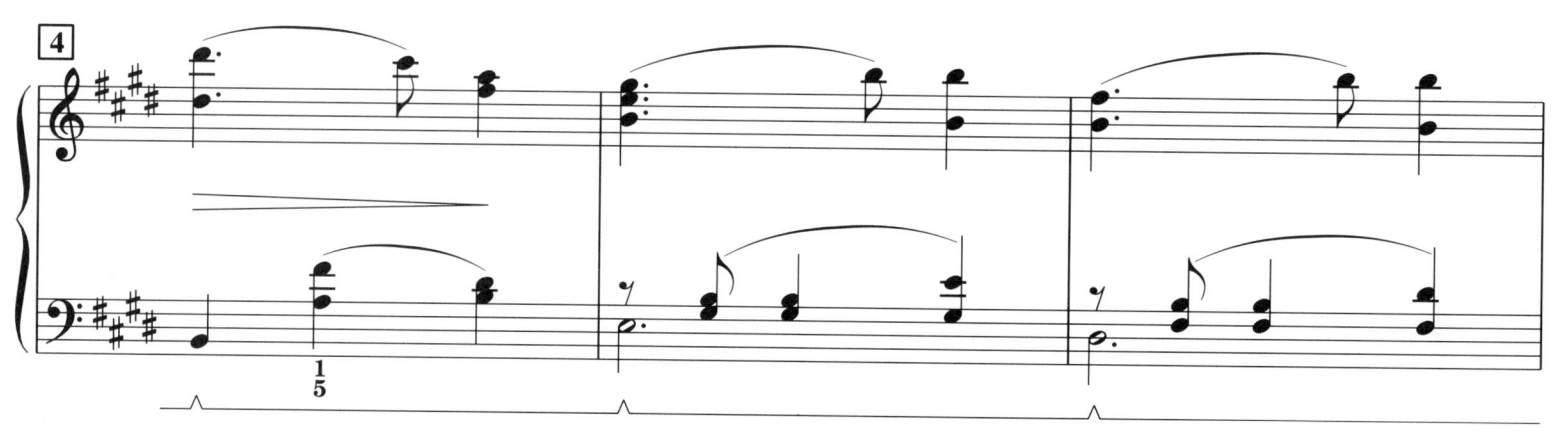

ⓐ Brahms left pedal marks for measures 3, 4, 7, 16, 17, 18 and 21. All other pedal indications are editorial.

Song of the Lark

Peter Ilyich Tchaikovsky (1840–1893)
Op. 39, No. 22

(a) Pedal indications are editorial. (b) Play the grace notes before the beat throughout the piece.

Bourrée en Rondeau [a]

Vincent d'Indy
(1851–1931)

[a] The folk tune used in this piece comes from the Cévennes Mountains in southern France.

Album Leaf

Claude Debussy (1862–1918)
L. 133

(a) Metronome marking is Debussy's.   (b) Pedal indications are editorial.

La fille aux cheveux de lin
(The Girl with the Flaxen Hair)

Claude Debussy (1862–1918)
L. 117:8

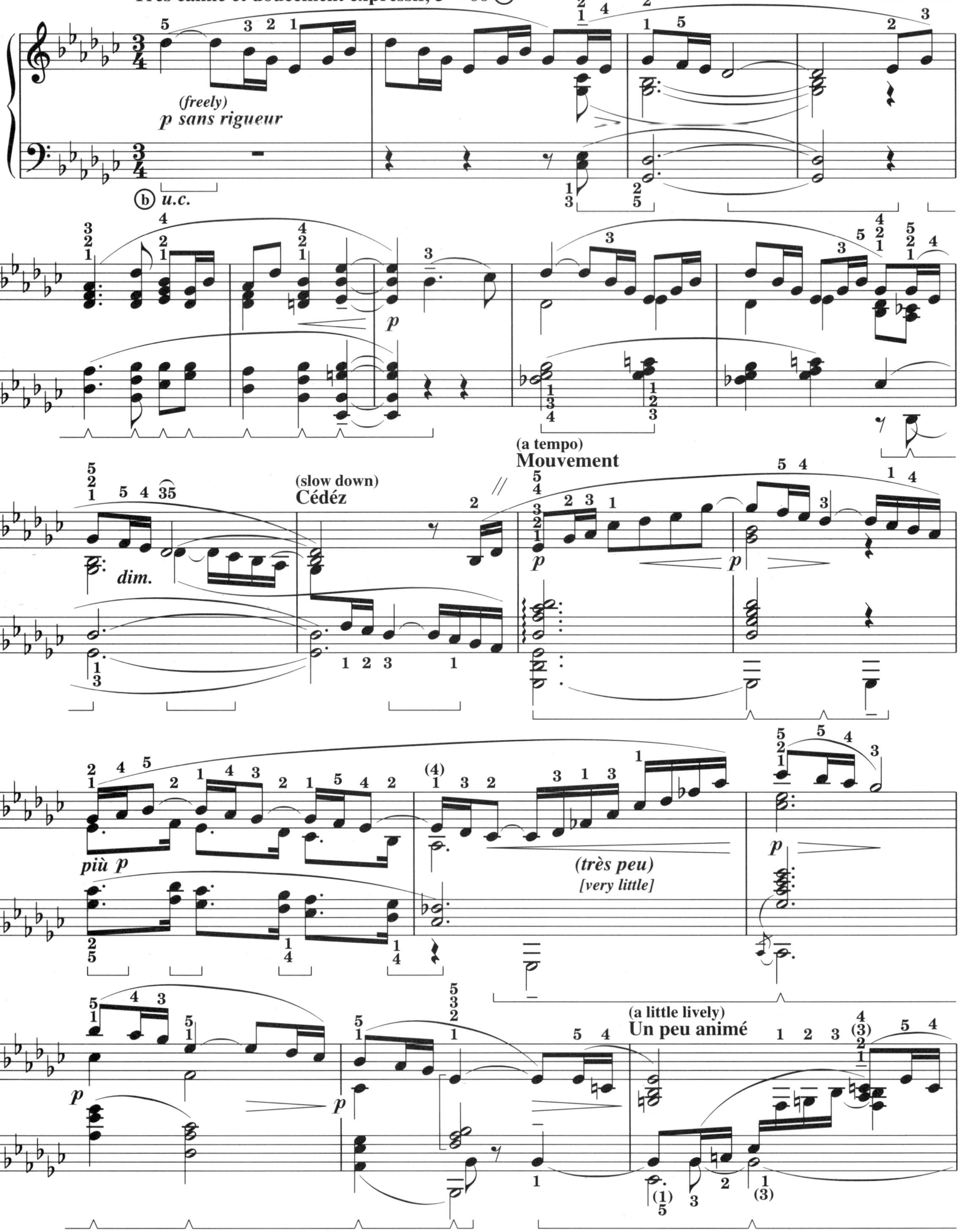

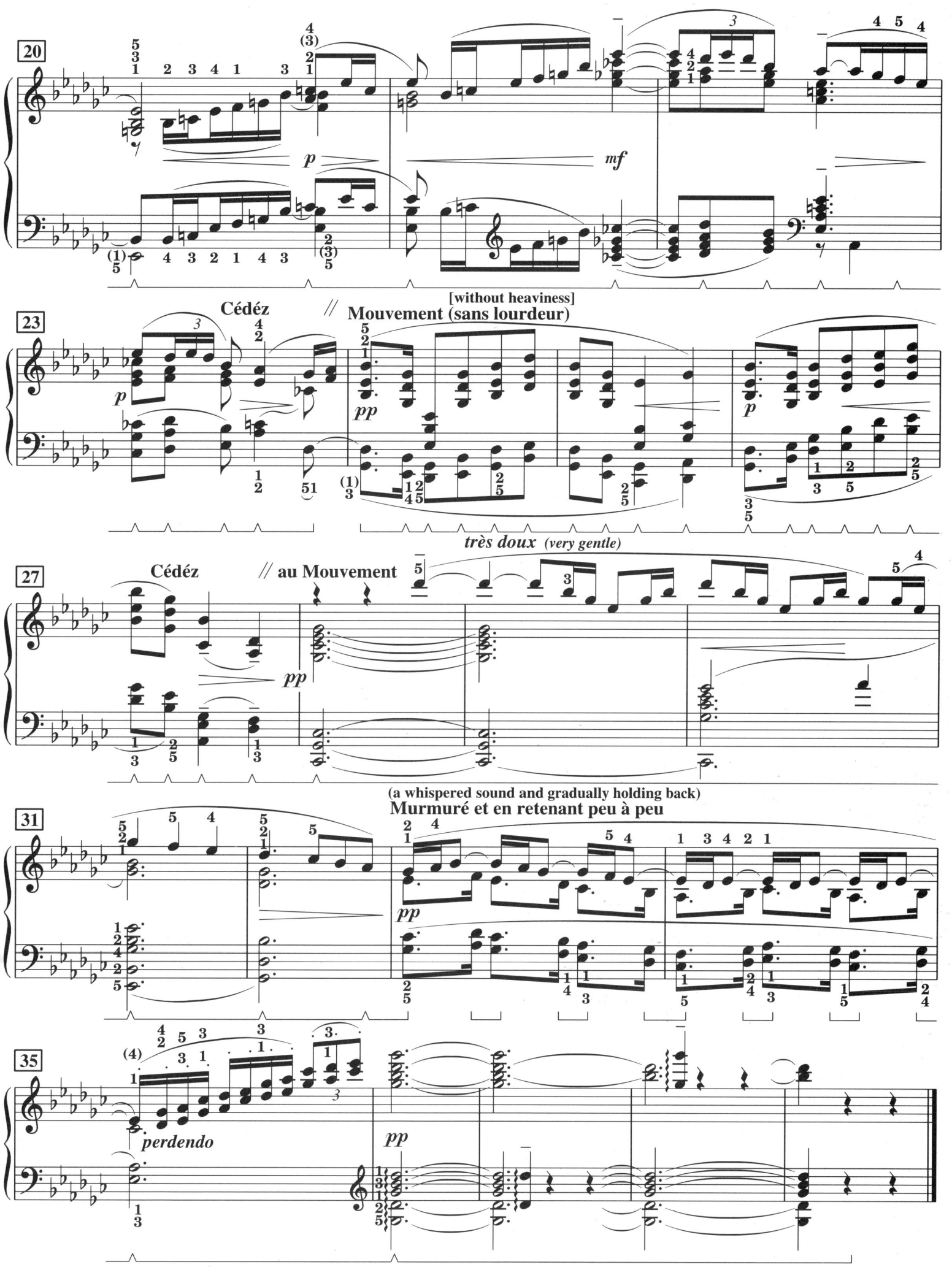

Danish Folk Tune

Carl Nielsen (1865–1931)
Op. 3, No. 1

ⓐ Pedal indications are editorial. ⓑ Play the grace notes before the beat.

The Tango
(Endless)

Erik Satie
(1866–1925)

May 5, 1914

ⓐ Satie frequently dispensed with measure lines. This piece is written in duple meter.
ⓑ The words tell a story but are not to be read during performance.
ⓒ The repeat sign means to repeat the piece as many times as desired (Endless).

The Bell of the Afternoon
from *Bocetos*

Enrique Granados
(1867–1916)

ⓐ Pedal indications are editorial.
ⓑ Play the grace notes before the beat throughout the piece.

Poetic Valse No. 6

Enrique Granados
(1867–1916)

ⓐ Pedal indications are editorial.
ⓑ Play the grace notes before the beat throughout the piece.

The Blacksmith

Samuel Maykapar (1867–1938)
Op. 8, No. 5

ⓐ Pedal indications are editorial.

Valse Viennoise
(Viennese Waltz)

Florent Schmitt (1870–1958)
Op. 32, No. 8

(a) Pedal indications are editorial.

Prelude in G Minor

Alexander Scriabin (1872–1915)
Op. 11, No. 22

ⓐ Metronome marking is Scriabin's.
ⓑ Pedal indications are editorial.

The Fairy Tale Princess

Ignacy Friedman (1882–1948)
Op. 76, No. 8

Bagatelle

Alexander Tcherepnin (1899–1977)
Op. 5, No. 1

ⓐ Metronome marking is Tcherepnin's.
ⓑ Pedal indications are editorial.

Chinese March [a]

Alexander Tcherepnin
(1899–1977)

[a] Title is editorial. Original was untitled.

The Jade Wheel Turns in the Dew [a]

Alexander Tcherepnin
(1899–1977)

[a] Title is editorial. Original was untitled.

Cat on a Swing

Aram Khachaturian
(1903–1978)

ⓐ Pedal indications are Khachaturian's.

By the Campfire

Dmitri Kabalevsky (1904–1987)
Op. 3/86, No.

(a) Pedal indications are editorial.

Who Will Win the Argument?

Dmitri Kabalevsky (1904–1987)
Op. 88, No. 2

Happy Birthday

Dmitri Shostakovich (1906–1975)
Op. 69, No.

ⓐ Pedal indications are editorial.